dr Slobodan D. Jovanović

ENGLESKI JEZIK ZA STUDENTE TEHNIKE

Drugo izdanje, izmenjeno i dopunjeno

dr Slobodan D. Jovanović

ENGLESKI JEZIK ZA STUDENTE TEHNIKE

Izbor tekstova i testova za usvajanje vokabulara

Drugo izdanje, izmenjeno i dopunjeno

Visoka tehnička škola
strukovnih studija

Beograd   2010.

Slobodan D. Jovanović
ENGLESKI JEZIK ZA STUDENTE TEHNIKE:
Izbor tekstova i testova za usvajanje vokabulara
Drugo izdanje, izmenjeno i dopunjeno

Recenzenti
prof. dr Ljiljana Jovković
Radmila Rakočević, prof.

Urednik
mr Mića Miletić

Izdavač
Visoka tehnička škola strukovnih studija
Beograd, Bulevar Zorana Đinđića 152a

Za Izdavača
prof. dr Miroslav Medenica,
direktor

Grafičko uređenje i štampa
Klasa, Beograd

Tiraž 200

ISBN 978-86-86691-27-9

SADRŽAJ

PREDGOVOR

Engleski jezik za studente tehnike je zbirka tekstova i testova čija su pojava i postojanje već dugo prizivani praktičnim zahtevima rada sa svima kojima je engleski jezik potreban na specifično nijansiranim poljima nauke i struke. Udžbenika opšteg jezika, gramatika i gramatičkih priručnika u današnjem trenutku je sve više, ali je sve prisutnije i insistiranje na vladanju što širim vokabularom različitih profila savremene tehnike. Upravo zbog toga korisnicima je trebalo ponuditi materijal namenjen upoznavanju, osvajanju i širenju rečnika osnovne fizike, matematike, elektrotehnike, kompjuterske tehnike i informatičkih tehnologija; tu su osnovni pojmovi i termini čije je poznavanje i shvatanje neophodno da bi se instalirao softverski program, ali i da bi se razumela kretanja na polju reklame i marketinga, isto kao i pojave u vezi s vasionom, iz domena opšte geografije i moreplovstva, s terena moćnih dostignuća nuklearne fizike, različitih prirodnih fenomena, ali i iz oblasti ekološke zaštite i staranja o planeti kao i poznavanja različitih sredstava i načina savremenih komunikacija. U vreme upadljivo oživljenih interesovanja za vokabular engleskog jezika i njegovo usvajanje i obogaćivanje u opštem smislu, razumljivo je snažna težnja da se njim što uspešnije vlada i u razuđivanju ka sve specifičnijim oblastima današnje tehnike.

Iz navedenih razloga zbirka koja se sada nudi ne izlaže i ne objašnjava eksplicitno gramatičku građu, već podrazumeva da svi njeni korisnici već vladaju nekim neophodnim nivoom strukture kao okvirom koji će se popunjavati kvalitetom u smislu što bogatijeg i što efikasnijeg rečnika, opšteg ali i postepeno sve stručnijeg. Zbog toga je prva celina koju ona donosi sastavljena od materijala iz priznatih savremenih publikacija, udžbeničkih, enciklopedijskih i popularnonaučnih, kao i od tekstova iz kvalitetne dnevne štampe, čime se obezbeđuju svežina i aktuelnost. Podrazumeva se da su svi tekstovi koji su uključeni pretrpeli minimalno neizbežno prilagođavanje potrebama ovog izdanja, makar samo u smislu neophodnih skraćivanja. Potom su predmet razmatranja brojne reči i izrazi, čije su upotrebe analizirane velikim brojem rečenica preuzetih iz najkvalitetnijih monolingvalnih rečnika. Prevoda nema, kako bi korisnici bili podstaknuti da se neprestano vraćaju tekstovima i rečeničnim primerima u cilju shvatanja suštine značenja i specifičnih grananja značenja i upotrebe. Na najvišim nivoima kvaliteta rada ova jednojezička priroda materijala osnovni je preduslov i za začinjanje razgovora na različite teme, opšte i stručne, čime se prilazi idealnoj kombinaciji vladanja rečnikom i njegove primene na komunikativan način.

Od možda još veće koristi i izvođačima nastave i studentima morao bi da je drugi deo ovog priručnika, sastavljen od testova s višečlanim izborom koji svojim brojem i sadržajem u potpunosti prate prethodno izložene tekstove. Ukupan broj rečenica/zadataka u njima, kao i ukupan broj reči i izraza izloženih u vidu ponuda za rešenja trebalo bi da posluže kao definitivna potvrda bogatstva leksičkog fonda engleskog jezika koji je ovde ponuđen. Pri tom se naročito misli na različite specifične upotrebe i značenja leksičkih jedinica na različitim poljima prirodnih nauka i tehnike.

Krećući se kroz materijal koji je ovde izložen, inventivan nastavnik ali i raspoložen i predan student shvatiće da tekstovi i testovi koji su ponuđeni služe prvenstveno olakšavanju i osavremenjavanju rada na rečniku engleskog jezika, ali da pri angažovanom i umešnom korišćenju mogu i te koliko da doprinesu obnavljanju i utvrđivanju znanja o njegovim pojedinim strukturama i opštim osobinama. Tekstovi upravo zbog toga i nisu sortirani ni po jednom od mogućih kriterijuma određivanja redosleda, već su izloženi s nadom da će biti shvaćeni kao dragoceni delovi jedne velike celine, kojoj neprestano treba têžiti. Duh takvog pristupa i takav način korišćenja materijala doneli bi onda puno obrazloženje velikom trudu i iskrenim dobrim namerama uloženim u njegovom prikupljanju i uobličavanju.

Beograd, jun 2009.   Slobodan Jovanović

PREDGOVOR DRUGOM IZDANJU

Praksa izvođenja nastave engleskog jezika sa studentima Visoke tehničke škole strukovnih studija tokom univerzitetske 2009/2010. godine donela je punu potvrdu upotrebne vrednosti ovako sastavljenog i plasiranog materijala. Knjiga je poslužila kao izvor tekstova čijom je obradom širen vokabular, ali i kao podloga za proveru znanja na kolokvijumima i ocenjivanje postignutog na pismenim ispitima. Veliki broj studenata je pri tom izražavao očekivanje da će im za budući rad biti ponuđen još bogatiji izbor tekstova. Ovo prerađeno i dopunjeno izdanje posvećeno je naročito takvim, vrednim i ambicioznim, korisnicima.

Beograd, jun 2010.   Autor

TEKSTOVI

2

What Every Pupil Should Know About Physics

- The atomic hypothesis … that all things are made of atoms.
- The connection between electricity and magnetism, revealed by Michael Faraday, which led to the electric motor and dynamo – the basis of all electrical power – and also to telephones, radio, television, and computers.
- Energy cannot be created or destroyed; it can only be converted from one form to another.
- The second law of thermodynamics – that spontaneous changes are accompanied by an increase of entropy, or disorder. Thus bedrooms and so on all tend to become untidy. Such events are preventable, but only if work is put in.
- The Copernican principle – the idea that our location is unlikely to be special. We started our thinking that the Earth was the centre of the universe. Nicolaus Copernicus convinced people that this was not true.
- The discovery of radioactivity gave us a glimpse of the microscopic world and has many practical applications, from dating of ancient artefacts to nuclear energy.
- The book of nature is written in the language of mathematics.
- Equal volumes of gases, at the same temperature and pressure, contain the same number of molecules.
- Sir Isaac Newton showed us how the laws that govern how things move on Earth, such as falling apples, govern how they move in the heavens too.

----

hypothesis; atoms
The atomic hypothesis says that all things are made of atoms.
reveal
The connection between electricity and magnetism was revealed by Michael Faraday.

dynamo
The waterfall turns a dynamo in the hydroelectric power station.
That man is a human dynamo who never seems to get tired.

convert
Energy can only be converted from one form to another.

thermodynamics
Thermodynamics is the science of the relations between heat and other forms of energy.
The principles of thermodynamics are used to design more efficient engines.

entropy
Spontaneous changes are accompanied by an increase of entropy. Such events are *preventable*.

untidy
Bedrooms all tend to become untidy.

Nicolaus Copernicus; Copernican; universe
Copernicus convinced people that the Earth was not the centre of the universe.
Our location in the universe is unlikely to be special.

radioactivity
The discovery of radioactivity has many practical applications.

artefacts
An artefact is a product of human workmanship (a tool, weapon, utensil, work of art), especially one of arch(a)eological interest.

language
The book of Nature is written in the language of mathematics.

govern; heavens
Newton showed us the laws that govern how things move in the heavens.

- **Give your own examples using:** *to put in, volume, molecule, preventable.*

Our Endangered Planet

Environmentalists organize Earth Day, April 22, to dramatize a simple message: The planet is threatened by a number of man-made ills, from acid forests and toxic landfills to global warming and ozone depletion.

Scientists are increasingly concerned about the waste industrial gases that are being discharged into the atmosphere and causing climatic change. What happens is that these gases, especially carbon dioxide from burning fossil fuel and the chlorofluorocarbons, form a kind of blanket around the earth, trapping the heat inside and gradually warming the earth's surface. This is popularly known as the *greenhouse effect.*

The effects of this global warming would vary from place to place. It would be largely beneficial to countries in the far north, but people living in warmer latitudes would suffer more severe droughts and resulting famine, desertification. Coastal cities might be flooded as the ice cap melts and raises sea levels.

The gases altering the natural composition of the atmosphere and thus increasing the danger of climatic change, are primarily carbon dioxide and the chlorofluorocarbons. Carbon dioxide is released when the fossil fuels: coal, oil and natural gas, burn. The chlorofluorocarbons are not produced naturally. They are industrial products widely used in refrigerators and aerosol sprays and stay in the atmosphere for a long time. Doubly destructive, the chlorofluorocarbons are also responsible for the depletion of the layer of ozone in the atmosphere. It is this layer of ozone that prevents dangerous ultraviolet light from reaching the earth's surface and increasing the risk of skin cancer.

Our endangered earth faces ecological problems of truly global magnitude. But if the problems are man-made, they must also be solved by man.

----

acid rains, acid forests
Acid rains contain impurities, usually from industrial pollution.
toxic landfills
The town's landfill site is quickly being used up.

global warming, greenhouse effect
The global warming may result from the greenhouse effect.
ozone depletion
Buying a car has depleted our funds.
discharge
Car exhausts discharge toxic gases into the air.
fossil fuel
Coal and oil are fossil fuels which will be used up one day.
chlorofluorocarbons
Chlorofluorocarbons, or CFCs, were developed in the 1930s.
Man-made CFCs are the main cause of ozone depletion in the stratosphere.
vary
The prices of fruit vary with the seasons.
latitude
Can you determine precisely London's latitude north of the equator? And what about
the city's *longitude*?
atmosphere
Atmospheric conditions influence the weather.
natural gas
Natural gas is found below ground, not manufactured.
refrigerators
A refrigerator is a container in which food and drink are kept cold.
Our new *fridge* has a freezer compartment at the top.
Most foods last longer if you *refrigerate* them.
aerosol sprays
Do you use an aerosol deodorant spray or a roll-on?
magnitude
We were frightened by the magnitude of the task.

- **Can you give your own explanations for:** *environmentalists, carbon dioxide, waste industrial gases, desertification?*

Alert over 4 million laptops that could burst into flames

Millions of computer users were warned recently that their laptops could burst into flames at any moment. In a dramatic admission, the world's largest computer firm, Dell, said 4.1 million machines were at risk from faulty batteries. A U.S. safety watchdog is urging owners, including thousands of British businesses, to stop using them immediately. It says the only way to ensure safety is to remove the battery and use the machine on mains power.

Dell has been ordered to recall all the lithium-ion batteries involved, which are made by Sony in Japan and China, in what is believed to be the biggest operation of its kind. Users will receive free replacements.

Apple Computer said it was investigating whether it could also be affected. The other major computer maker, Hewlett-Packard, does not use Sony batteries.

At least six Dell laptops have already burst into flames and there are unconfirmed reports of many more being affected. At a conference in Japan, a laptop was photographed exploding into flames in what could have been a deadly incident. One onlooker said: 'The damn thing was on fire and produced explosions for more than five minutes.'

A man from Singapore told an Australian newspaper that his laptop caught fire while he was working late in the office. He said: 'White smoke began to pour out of the machine, completely filling up the room. There were flames coming up the sides.'

It emerged that this is the fourth problem Dell has experienced with overheating batteries in the last five years. Dell was told by the U.S. Consumer Product Safety Commission to recall faulty batteries in October 2000, May 2001 and December 2005. A total of 333,000 batteries were involved.

----

alert
A siren will sound the alert if there is an air raid.
We must be on the alert for any sudden attack by the enemy.

watchdog
A good watchdog barks at strangers.
That journalist acts as the consumers' watchdog.
businesses
She runs her own hairdressing business.
mains power
Until we were connected to the mains, we relied on a borehole for water.
replacement
Computers have replaced typewriters in most offices.
be affected
Failing eyesight will affect his work.
We *were* deeply affected by the news of his death.
onlooker
One onlooker was injured in the shootout.
pour out of
We saw the smoke pour out of the chimney.
fill up
Please fill up the tank with petrol.
emerge
The situation changed with the *emergence* of new facts.

- **Can you now make sentences with:** *warn, dramatic, be at risk; Consumer Product Safety Commission?*

8

Branches of Engineering

Engineering has been defined as the art of directing the great sources of power in nature for the use and convenience of man. In its modern form the practice of engineering involves men, money, materials, machines and energy. It is differentiated from science because it is primarily concerned with how to apply and direct to useful ends the basic natural phenomena which scientists discover and formulate into acceptable theories. Engineering therefore requires above all the creative imagination to innovate useful applications to natural phenomena. It is always dissatisfied with present methods and equipment. It seeks newer, cheaper, better means of using natural sources of energy and materials to improve man's standard of living and to diminish laborious toil.

Historically speaking, modern engineering started with the invention of the steam engine (Denis Papin, James Watt). This machine first transformed the textile trade, then, gradually, the other trades, transportation and, finally, agriculture (the Industrial Revolution).

Traditionally there were two divisions or disciplines – military engineering and civil engineering. As man's knowledge of natural phenomena grew and the potential civil applications became more complex, the civil engineering discipline tended to become more and more specialized. The practising engineer began to restrict his operations into narrower channels. For instance, civil engineering came to be concerned primarily with static structures, such as dams, bridges and buildings, whereas mechanical engineering split off to concentrate on dynamic structures, such as machinery and engines. Similarly, mining engineering became concerned with the discovery of and removal from geological structures of metalliferous ore bodies, whereas metallurgical engineering involved extraction and refinement of the metals from the ores. From the practical applications of electricity and chemistry, electrical and chemical engineering arose. This fractionating process continued as narrower specialization became more prevalent.

----

engineering
Engineering is the practical application of science to the design, building, and use of machines, constructions, etc.
My brother is an engineer and is involved with road construction.

involve
This job involves a high degree of accuracy.
The plot of the film is too involved to relate so you'll have to go and see it for yourself.
phenomenon, phenomena
The phenomenon of an erupting volcano is an awesome spectacle.
A comet orbiting close to Earth is a rare phenomenon.
seek
Hikers often seek shelter from the rain in these caves.
She is seeking fame in the world of art.
toil
Farmers toil all day in the fields.
The overloaded car toiled up the hill.
trade
He is an electrician by trade; his wife is a teacher by profession.
A plumber is a tradesman.
specialized
Use specialized/specialised tools for that job!
restrict
The poor have to restrict their spending to essentials.
I suggest you restrict yourself to your studies and forget about watching movies!
dams
A dam is a barrier to hold back water. The large stream was dammed at the gorge.
You shouldn't dam up your emotions all the time!
split off
An iceberg split *away/off* from the main mass of the glacier.
The militants have split *away/off* to form their own political party.
metalliferous
The metalliferous mine was what this small town once started growing around.
Metallurgy includes the study of separating metals from their ores.
extraction
To extract means to take or get something with force or difficulty.
Freshly extracted orange juice is delicious.
He's an American of German extraction.
refinement
The refinement of oil occurs at the refinery.
This machine comes with an alarm and other refinements.
fractionating process
Fraction is a small part, portion or amount.
½ is a vulgar or simple fraction and 0.5 is a decimal.
1½ is an improper fraction.

- **Try to give your own examples using**: *shelter, plumber, juice, vulgar, improper.*

Running scared

Bill gates displays a paranoid tendency common among technology industry billionaires. "In this business, by the time you realise you're in trouble, it's too late to save yourself," he once said. "Unless you're running scared all the time, you're gone."

Tech fashions – and fortunes – shift with great speed. The Microsoft Mr. Gates founded might not yet be on the scrapheap of history but, as its unsolicited takeover offer for Yahoo makes clear, even seemingly dominant companies find it hard to keep pace in the latest and most promising tech markets.

A decade ago, who could have imagined that the feared monopolist of the software business would be so roundly beaten in online search and advertising by Google that it would have to mount a hostile bid for another distant also-ran to try to catch up. Predicting where the next big disruptive change in the technology industry will come from is a perilous business. Google's rise has been as much a result of its business model innovation as its technological supremacy. By using advertising to support its internet services, it may eventually be able to pull the rug from under Microsoft in more traditional software markets.

It seems a fair bet, though, that some of the biggest fortunes will continue to be made in Google's area of focus: finding and manipulating information gathered from the world wide web. To hear the optimists describe it, a new wave of technology is on the way – the level of computer-generated reasoning. It may still take 15 years or more to be fully realised, but between now and then lies a series of breakthroughs that will revolutionise the way we draw information from the web. This technology draws its inspiration, and some of its techniques, from a field that has provided more than its fair share of disappointments over the years: artificial intelligence (AI).

----

running scared
He was scared stiff at the thought of making a speech.

billionaire
Billion is a thousand million.
In Britain, a million million is now called a trillion.
disruptive
That naughty child is disruptive in class.
perilous
Perilous is something that brings a great danger.
rise
Unemployment is on the rise, unfortunately.
supremacy
The Romans had political supremacy 2,000 years ago.
to pull a rug from under...
This car will pull the trailer.
The pop star is a crowd puller.
a fair bet
It's an even bet whether she will come or not.
It's a fair price for a car of that age.
world wide web
The World Wide Web lets you communicate worldwide via your computer.
artificial intelligence – AI
Artificial flowers are pretty, but they have no scent.

- **Your turn now! Make examples using:** *tech, shift, scrapheap, keep pace, monopolist, one's share of (disappointments).*

The Future of Cyberspace

In the last thirty years, the Internet has grown dramatically. In 1983, there were only 200 computers connected to the Internet; now there are over 50 million and this growth is clearly going to continue.

Some experts are pessimistic about the future. One worry is the activities of cybercriminals. Even now, young hackers can get into the computers of banks and governments. In the future, cyberterrorists may 'attack' the world's computers, cause chaos, and make planes and trains crash.

Many people, however, are optimistic about the future of the Internet. Already, users can buy books, find out about holiday offers, book tickets, and get all sorts of information from the Internet. It is clear that in the years to come we are going to see a true explosion of shopping on the Internet. Many also believe that, in the future, we will get entertainment from the Net and that television will probably disappear. The postal service may also disappear with the increasing use of e-mail.

Some specialists see our future in virtual reality – the use of computers with sounds and images that make you feel as if you are in a real situation. Virtual reality will become part of modern life, and some experts even see people living and working in a virtual world. We will work in virtual offices, shop in virtual supermarkets, and we will even study in virtual schools.

----

cybercriminals, cyberterrorists
Cybernetics is concerned with comparing human brain with machines and electronic   devices.
cyber space
The Internet is the gateway to the world of cyberspace.
affect
Do you feel that your life is affected by the use of computer and the Internet?
dramatically
We have seen dramatic changes during the 20th century.
Many things changed dramatically in that period.
hackers
A hacker managed to access a computer system with top-secret information.

crash

I can't do any work because the computer has crashed again.

There was a crash on the freeway between two trucks.

Engine failure forced the pilot to crash-land.

e-mail, E-mail, email

She sent a message to her colleagues overseas by E-mail/e-mail/email.

modern

Drug abuse is a serious problem of modern times.

Older people tend to criticize the modern generation.

Modern advertising methods have boosted sales.

explosion of shopping

More people are living longer causing a population explosion.

- **Try to make your own examples using:** *make sth. crash, virtual reality, image, modern, fashionable.*

THE LAWS OF MOTION AND UNIVERSAL GRAVITATION

Sir Isaac Newton (1642-1727), one of the most profound scientists of all time, interpreted and correlated many observations in mechanics and combined the results into three fundamental laws of motion.

First law of motion. A body at rest remains at rest, and a body in motion continues to move at constant speed along a straight line, unless there is a resultant force acting upon the body. The first part of the law is evident from everyday experience; for instance, a book placed on a table remains at rest. The second part of the law is more difficult to visualize; it states that if a body is set into motion and left to itself, it keeps on moving without the action of any further force. This statement is correct; the body would continue to move without any reduction of velocity if no force acted upon it. However, experience shows that a retarding force is always present in the nature of friction. If friction could be eliminated entirely, a body once set into motion on a level surface would continue to move indefinitely with undiminished velocity. Therefore, uniform motion is a natural condition and maintains itself without the action of a resultant force. It is interesting to note that whether a body is at rest or moving with constant speed along a straight line, its acceleration is zero. Hence the first law of motion means that a body accelerates only while some resultant force acts upon it.

Second law of motion. The acceleration of a body takes place in the direction of the resultant force acting upon it; the acceleration is directly proportional to the resultant force and inversely proportional to the mass of the body. In general, the greater the resultant force and the smaller the mass, the greater is the acceleration.

Third law of motion. For every action there is an equal and opposite reaction, and the two are directed along the same straight line. In this statement, the term *action* means the force that one body exerts on a second body, and *reaction* means the force that the second body exerts on the first. It should be noted that the action and reaction are never exerted on the same object. Thus, action and reaction, although equal and opposite, can never balance each other. Consequently, the first and second laws deal with forces on a single body; the third law deals with the mutual forces between two bodies.

Law of universal gravitation. Newton also showed that every particle in the universe attracts every other particle, and explained how this attraction is affected by the masses of the particles and the distances separating them. The law reads: Each particle of matter attracts every other particle with a force that is directly proportional to the product of their masses and inversely proportional to the square of the distance between them.

----

profound
This is a profound book, not many people will understand it.
We were in awe of Einstein because of his profundity.
correlated
Correlation is a mutual relationship between things.
You must correlate the evidence with the facts in order to convince the judge.
fundamental
His ideas are fundamentally sound even if he sometimes says outrageous things.
a resultant force
They turned up the amplifiers so the resultant noise was deafening.
The company had to pay for damage resulting from its negligence.
visualize
Can you visualize/visualise what life would be like in 100 years?
Visuals in the next programme may upset viewers!
velocity
A puma attains an astonishing velocity (speed) over short distances.
a retarding force
If the clock is too fast, retard the mechanism!
Too little sun will retard a plant's growth.
friction
Friction is the rubbing of one thing against another.
There is little friction between the wheels of a car and icy roads.
proportional; inversely proportional
Inverse proportion is a relation between two quantities where one increases in proportion as the other decreases.
The figure 9 looks like an inverted 6, doesn't it?
2 is to 3 as 12 is to 18 is a statement of proportion.
universal
English is becoming a universal language spoken on all continents.
Nuclear war would be universally disastrous.
particle
Even a tiny particle of dust could make him sneeze.
product
Factories produce a wide range of consumer goods from raw materials.
Twelve is the product of 3 x 4.
A pure solution can be the product of chemical distillation.
square
Square is the product of a number multiplied by itself.
3 x 3 = 9, therefore 9 is the square of 3.
4 squared is 16.

- **Think up your own sentences with:** *separate, square, triangle, circle, multiply, divide, add, subtract.*

Mars, the Red Planet

Mars, named after the Roman god of war, is called the Red Planet because it actually looks red. But Mars is not only an extremely beautiful planet. For a long time this question has fascinated us – 'Is there life on Mars?', our next-door neighbour. Venus is actually nearer but has a very hostile environment, covered in clouds of poison gas and with temperatures of up to 500 deg. Centigrade. Mars is cooler, has an atmosphere made up of carbon dioxide and its gravity is a third of that on Earth. Mars has two moons, Phobos and Deimos. The surface is covered with craters and huge volcanoes, also canyons and valleys that were probably made in the past by the presence of water on the planet.

Towards the end of the nineteenth century improved telescopes meant that astronomers could start to observe the surface of the planet. The Italian astronomer Schiaparelli saw channels on the surface and this caused enormous interest. Unfortunately, his work was mistranslated into English and people thought that 'canals' had been found. This triggered speculation about the possibility of life on Mars and 'Martians' entered science fiction for the first time. In H. G. Wells' famous book *The War of the Worlds* of 1898, Martians are highly developed creatures that try to take over planet Earth.

The first probe to get near Mars was *Mariner 4*, which flew past the planet in 1964 and took photos of it. After that, there were several failures, with probes crashing on landing or failing to go into orbit. The big breakthrough came with *Pathfinder*, which successfully landed on July 4, 1997 and sent back spectacular photos of the surface of Mars. These photos and the six-wheel vehicle which explored the area sparked great public interest. A more recent probe to be sent was the *Mars Odyssey*, launched in April 2001, with the task to orbit the planet and provide communications for future missions.

Another period of great interest in the planet was caused by the finding of a meteorite from Mars in Antarctica. In 1996, the American space agency NASA declared that it proved that there had been life on Mars in the form of tiny bacteria. The claim was later dismisssed by other scientists, but another study in 2001 confirmed that the meteorite did contain chains of crystals that could only be made by living organisms. This has sparked renewed speculation about whether there is life on the planet now.

The future of the exploration of Mars? In 2014, the first return mission is planned, which means that a space probe will bring back to Earth samples of Martian rock and soil. After that, there might be the first crewed mission to Mars. At the moment, a manned mission to Mars is right at the edge of our technological capacities. There are many problems because of the length of the return journey which would take about two years. But a manned mission could explore the planet further and even analyse the possibilities for human settlement on the planet. To sum up – in many ways Mars is our new frontier.

----

environment
We need laws to prevent further pollution of the environment.
atmosphere
The Earth's atmosphere contains oxygen.
Atmospherics are electrical disturbances in the atmosphere, and radio interference produced by them.
carbon dioxide
Plants give off the gas carbon dioxide.
craters
Nothing grew in the crater left by the explosion.
volcanoes
Lava poured from the rim of the volcano's crater.
canyons
The river flowed through the canyon. A canyon is a deep gorge, a ravine.
channel
A channel is a broad strait, especially between two seas.
canal
Canal is an artificial waterway, or one made by altering a river, etc.
We are going to canalize/canalise the stream to ensure better irrigation.
crash
Motorcyclists must wear crash helmets to protect their heads.
His business crashed in spite of his hard work.
breakthrough
Breakthrough is an important discovery or development.
chains of crystals
He used a chain saw to cut down the tree.
A chain smoker lights up one cigarette after another.
Salt crystallizes through evaporation.
return mission, crewed mission, manned mission
Crew are the people manning a ship, aircraft, etc., or a team of workers.

- **Do you understand the words:** *hostile, gravity, telescope, mistranslate, explore, orbit, meteorite, trigger, speculation; to spark interest*?

MOST COMMON PROBLEMS WITH R/C VEHICLES

1. WEAK BATTERIES: Make certain all batteries are fresh. If your vehicle is designed to accommodate Ni-Cd rechargeable batteries, make certain they are properly charged. In other cases use high quality alkaline batteries.

2. INCORRECT BATTERY INSTALLATION: Frequently, batteries are installed in the reverse position or they are not making good contact with the battery terminals.

3. BATTERY FAILURE: Make certain the vehicle is turned off when not in use. Also, be sure to turn off the transmitter.

4. RANGE: Sometimes, the vehicle is driven beyond radio signal range causing loss of control. Range on most small radio-controlled vehicles is approximately 30' to 50' unless specifically designed for long range, high-speed racing.

5. RUNNING TIME: Alkaline batteries generally do not last longer than 25 to 40 minutes. If driving continuously, batteries must be replaced, unless vehicle is specifically designed to use Ni-Cd rechargeable batteries. If so, these types of batteries must be recharged.

6. INTERFERENCE: Sometimes erratic behaviour or loss of control of vehicle is due to being in an area interference sources. Such sources are CB radios, microwave transmitters, cordless telephones, wireless communication or security systems, or high voltage transformers or even certain buildings. If you encounter this type of interference, change to a better location to drive your vehicle.

7. SAME FREQUENCIES: Avoid radio controlled vehicles driving on your same frequency. Wait until their transmitter is turned off before you start to drive.

8. ABUSE: Handle your vehicle delicately and avoid driving into obstacles. Drive on dry, smooth, flat clean surfaces, unless your vehicle is specifically designed for "off-road" use. Avoid damp areas.

9. SERVICE: Do not return the car to the store where purchased. For problems of service, please contact the Repair Center.

----

rechargeable batteries, alkaline batteries, Ni-Cd batteries
I couldn't start the car because the battery was flat.
Fire from the enemy battery halted the soldiers' advance.
We will need to recharge the car's flat battery.
A hard-working man needs a holiday to recharge his batteries.
terminal
Attach the wire to the positive terminal.
A parachute reduces the terminal velocity of a falling body.
turn on/off
Don't forget to turn off the oven when the cake is ready!
Turn off the highway when you see the signpost to the airport.
After the traffic lights, take the third turn-off to the left.
Turn on the taps to run the bath, please!
Don't turn on her! She was only joking.
Blondes turn him on.
range; long range
At that moment the aircraft came within my range of vision.
We followed the river ranging to the west.
control
She lost control of herself and flew into a temper.
Who is in control here?
An air-traffic controller monitors aircraft from a radar screen.
interference
You mustn't let your hobbies interfere with your work!
Intense sun-spot activity can cause interference on radio.
erratic behaviour
That clock is very erratic – sometimes fast, sometimes slow.
microwave transmitters
They managed to transform the dilapidated house into a lovely home.
Use a step-down transformer with a 110V shaver in a 220V plug.
A microwave can pass through solid materials.
cordless telephones
We need a long cord to connect the heater to the power point.
Cordless screwdrivers are very convenient as they can be moved around easily.
wireless
The wiring in this house needs to be replaced.

- **Can you give some sentences to illustrate the meanings of:** *CB radios, a wireless set, high voltage transformers, frequencies, obstacles, damp?*

The Analytical Mind – A Perfect Computer

The human mind can be considered to have three major divisions. First, there is the *analytical mind*; second, there is the *reactive mind*; and third, there is the *somatic mind.*

Consider the analytical mind as a computing machine. This is analogy because the analytical mind, while it behaves like a computing machine, is yet more fantastically capable than any computing machine ever constructed and infinitely more elaborate. It could also be called the "computational mind". This mind may live in the prefrontal lobes (portion of the brain directly behind the forehead) – there is some hint of that – but this is a problem of structure, and nobody really knows about structure. So we shall call this computational part of the mind the "analytical mind" because it analyzes data.

The analytical mind shows various evidences of being an organ, but as we know in this age so little of structure, the full structural knowledge of the analytical mind must come after we know what it does. And it is known and can be proven with ease that the analytical mind, be it one organ of the body or several, behaves as you would expect any good computing machine to behave.

What would you want in a computing machine? The action of the analytical mind – or analyzer – is everything anyone could want from the best computer available. It can and does do all the tricks of a computer. And over and above that, it directs the building of computers. And it is as thoroughly right as any computer ever was. The analytical mind is not just a *good* computer, it is a *perfect* computer. It never makes a mistake. It cannot err in any way so long as a human being is reasonably intact (unless something has carried away a piece of his mental equipment). The analytical mind is incapable of error, and it is so certain that it is incapable of error that it works out everything on the basis that it cannot make an error. If a person says, "I cannot add," he either means that he has never been taught to add or that he has an aberration about adding. It does not mean that there is anything wrong with the analytical mind. A computer is just as good as the data on which it operates and no better. Aberration, then, arises from the nature of the data offered to the analytical mind as a problem to be computed.

----

analytical mind; reactive mind, somatic mind
He is a chemical analyst.

An analytical report was submitted.
An analysis of the water showed it to be polluted with chemicals.
In the final/last analysis I think he was at fault.
Analytical mind is the best analyzer possible.
Mind is the human faculty which enables us to think, feel, etc.
Keep your mind (concentration) on what you are doing!
Her mind (intelligence, intellect) is brilliant.
computer
Computer programs are also known as software.
Computer is an electronic device that makes high-speed calculations and records, processes, arranges, stores and retrieves data.
division
There was a sharp division of opinions.
Division is easy if you have a calculator.
infinitely
Peace is infinitely preferable to war!
The universe contains an infinite number of stars.
prefrontal lobes
A lobe is a rounded section (or projection) of certain organs in the body, especially the lungs or brain.
structure
The TV mast is a tall structure.
The bridge is old but still structurally sound.
Structure is something which is constructed of many parts.
thoroughly
Please study this topic thoroughly!
The thoroughness of his research is impressive!
incapable
She is such a gentle person that she is incapable of violence.
That manager was dismissed because he was quite incapable.
error
Their facts are correct, but their conclusion is erroneous.
I have erred (formal) in my estimation of his capabilities.
aberration
Drugs are the cause of his recent aberrant behaviour.
She burnt the toast in a moment of aberration.
data
Data are relevant facts and information, statistical material, etc.
The data is/are still being processed.
Feed the data into the computer!

- **What about making some examples with:** *human faculty, TV mast, dismiss, analyzer, datum/data, feed?*

HOW STATISTICS CAN FOOL YOU

'There are three kinds of lies: lies, damned lies, and statistics' – Mark Twain

You are likely to come across statistics from two sources: learned publications and the advertisement columns of your daily newspaper. They differ considerably in many respects, but they have this much in common: neither of them is likely to be composed of flat lies. That is to say, if a scientific commission tells you that a thousand mice contaminated with some disgusting compound died, then – whatever may be the value of the information – they almost certainly did.

Statistics can be misleading in a number of ways: first and foremost, they are utterly valueless unless they cover a large and random selection of cases. Suppose, for instance, you are told that during one year in a certain hospital one hundred per cent of unvaccinated patients died of smallpox whereas among vaccinated patients there was not a single fatality, you will probably draw some very far-reaching conclusions. But let us suppose you now learn that this hospital during the year under review admitted precisely two cases of smallpox. That will surely give you pause. A hundred per cent sounds very large indeed; but when considering only one patient of each category it is just one more than nought per cent: the difference is statistically speaking not significant.

Statistics is a branch – and by no means the easiest branch – of mathematics. The normal use of statistics is to indicate trends. The statistician finds (or rather selects) two or more phenomena which occur, or increase, more or less simultaneously. If these phenomena are to be dealt with statistically, the essential preliminary is to establish some causal connection between them. Without that any statistical treatment is sheer waste of time if not dishonest.

Statistics when designed to show that A causes B can mislead you in at least three ways. We will take it that A and B do tend to occur (or to increase) simultaneously. Of course this may well be because A causes B. But may it not equally well be because B causes A, or because both A and B are effects of a perhaps unsuspected cause C? Or may it not be purely coincidental?

----

to come across sth.
If you come across my keys, please let me know!

To come across also means to convey a general impression – He comes across as a thoroughly decent person.

To come across is also a slang term meaning to provide what is wanted – Do you think he will come across with the money?

statistics

Statistics is one of her courses at university.

Statistical information is used to measure population growth.

column

Can you add up these columns of figures?

Column is a vertical section of a page, especially in a newspaper or magazine.

The article continues in the first column of the next page.

Column is also a particular section of a newspaper – Have you read the editorial column in The Daily Mail today?

flat lies

The answer's no, and that's flat!

I'm flat broke!

compound

Compound is a combination of two or more different substances, a mixture.

The chemical compound of water is two parts of hydrogen to one part of oxygen.

A compound of asphalt and gravel is used for road-surfacing.

misleading

The advertisement was misleading – inaccurate, confusing, deceptive.

He misled me into thinking he was wealthy.

random selection

The winning numbers were picked at random from a hat.

fatality

There were many fatalities in the train crash.

far-reaching

The new tax legislation will have a far-reaching effect.

indicate trends

A trend is a general direction or tendency.

The trendsetter starts a fashion that others copy.

causal connection

Dirt is the cause of the infection.

We don't know what caused the accident.

sheer

By sheer (complete, utter) luck I found the ring that I had lost.

coincidental

Coincidence is a remarkable occurrence of similar events or circumstances.

What a coincidence!

- **Now try to make sentences of your own using:** *slang, a slang term, university courses, learned, editorial column, smallpox, differ, trendsetters, phenomena.*

A Landmark Science Fiction Film

When *2001: Space Odyssey* originally came out in 1968, a lot of people did not like it – they couldn't make it out, they found it strange and confusing. At the Hollywood premiere of the film a lot of people walked out, including the actor Rock Hudson. However, it gradually became very popular, particularly among young people.

The film is based on a story by Arthur C. Clarke and was directed by the American film director Stanley Kubrick. The film is very original, it is totally unlike most science fiction films. There is very little action or dialogue, but Kubrick made up for it by spectacular photography, the visual effects are fantastic. The music is also brilliant. At the beginning of the film, Kubrick uses a piece by Richard Strauss to get across the mystery of the scene. Another famous piece of music that is used is Johann Strauss' waltz 'The Blue Danube', played deliberately slowly.

It is not easy to explain what the film is about. It could be said that it is to do with an alien civilisation, but you never actually see any aliens. The beginning of the film is set in prehistoric times, about four million years ago. It is about a group of ape-men who find an enormous monolith, a sort of big black block. It is really a strange kind of machine that has been sent to Earth by an advanced alien civilisation. The next part of the film happens four million years later in the year 2001. Two strange, black monoliths have been found on the Moon and a scientist goes there to investigate it.

The third part of the film is about a trip to Jupiter. Five men are on a space mission to that planet. Three of them are in hibernation and the other two, Dave and Frank, are looking after the ship. Or rather the new supercomupter, HAL 9000, is looking after it. However, after a while, the computer begins to act strangely. HAL detects a serious problem in the spaceship. It says that the ship's communication systems are going to fall. Then, the 9000 computer back on Earth says that there is nothing wrong and that HAL has made a mistake. Dave and Frank begin to get worried about HAL and talk about disconnecting it. What they do not know is that HAL can hear them talking. HAL is the only one on the ship who knows the real mission and he must do everything he can to stop the men from disconnecting him...

----

landmark
That Tower is a tall landmark on the skyline.
The fall of the Berlin wall was a momentous landmark in the history of Germany.
science fiction
Star Trek is a well-known television sci-fi series.
His collection of science fiction numbers over 1,000 films and books.
Odyssey
He is on a spiritual odyssey, studying all the great religions.
originally
Originally, before the rain, we planned to go jogging.
There are many theories about the origin of life on Earth.
Many rivers originate in the mountains.
make sth. out
We can't make out why the firm is firing its technical staff.
He has such illegible handwriting that no one can make it out.
premiere
The premiere/première of the new play was a huge success.
The film was premiered/premièred at the Cannes Festival.
spectacular
We tried to cope with the spectacular increase in sales.
photography
Photography is a very popular hobby.
A photograph is a print from a negative.
civilisation
To civilize/civilise is to bring education and enlightenment.
The civilization/civilisation of ancient Greece produced architecture of lasting beauty.
monolith
Stonehenge is a famous example of a monolithic monument.
investigate
That matter is under investigation.
Sherlock Holmes investigated many ingenious crimes.
space mission
Our country's trade mission visited China.
The president sent his deputy on a special mission.
hibernation
Brown bears go into hibernation in winter; they hibernate in winter.
detect
Do I detect a note of sarcasm in your voice?
disconnect
There must be something wrong with the phone, we've been disconnected.
You should disconnect the TV before working on it!

- **Can you make sentences illustrating the meanings of:** *staff, technical staff, festival, hobby, trip, hibernation, detect?*

WHAT MACHINES CAN, AND CAN NOT, DO

Anybody who talks about a Thinking Machine either doesn't know what thinking is or else doesn't know what a machine is. A machine is a tool operated by a man; it will, if it is in sound working order, carry out its instructions efficiently – as efficiently as its operator directs it. Machines, we are told, don't 'make mistakes'. Of course they don't; they don't make anything. If any errors have crept into this text (a not impossible hypothesis) there will be little use in telling the indignant readers that the keyboard has failed. Keyboards don't make spelling mistakes; but those who type sometimes do.

It would be ridiculous to deny that machinery, and particularly electronic machinery, has in the recent years made fantastic progress; but there has not been and never will be a breakthrough into conscious and volitional activity. An electronic computer is, when you get down to fundamentals, only an improved abacus.

A great deal of the current misunderstanding about machinery arises from the misuse of metaphors. We say that machines have 'memories' and that they can make 'decisions'. What we mean in fact is that they can store information (as can a filing cabinet) and that they respond to stimuli. The thermostat is a useful and valuable invention; but nobody would venture to suggest that it 'decides' to switch off the heat when a certain temperature is reached.

Electronic machinery works at lightning speed and can reply in a matter of seconds to questions that might engage a team of mathematicians for years; but it can deal only with a restricted range of questions, and it has to be 'programmed'. It never starts from scratch; information must be fed in before it can be given out. Also, since the machine works on impulses, the only answers it can give to any question are 'yes' and 'no' corresponding to the positive and negative states of 'on' and 'off'. Particularly in the field of mathematics, information can be obtained from a machine only if the question is first framed in mathematical language. No machine can solve a 'problem'.

----

age
We live in the age of computers.

outward / inward
An inward curve is called concave.
The door opens inwards, not outwards.
The branches of the tree spread outwards.
Whatever he feels, a captain must appear outwardly confident.
He stowed away on an outward bound cargo ship.
carry out
It is important to carry out all the instructions.
indignant
She was indignant when accused of shoplifting.
The scandal aroused public indignation.
conscious
She regained consciousness soon after the operation.
fundamentals
Master the fundamentals of swimming before you try diving!
abacus
Some Chinese businessmen still use the abacus in preference to a modern calculator.
store information
An educated person has a mind well stored with facts.
Store away your winter clothes in summer!
stimuli
Exercise will stiumulate the blood circulation.
thermostat
A thermostat regulates the heat of the oven so it stays constant.
venture
You can't succeed without taking risks: nothing venture, nothing gain.
We didn't feel like venturing out into the cold, dark night.
switch off
Where is the switch for the lights?
The signalman switched the train onto the other track.
start from scratch
We had to start from scratch after our CDs were stolen.
Luckily he escaped without a scratch.
feed information
Leaking oil fed the flames.
Can you feed this information into the computer?
The feed tray of a photocopier holds the blank paper.
impulses
Think first, and curb your impulsiveness!
On impulse, she phoned her brother, who was in Germany.

- **Can you tell the difference between** *conscious, consciousness, conscience,* **cons***cientious?* **Give some examples using:** *machine, machinery, tool, hypothesis, keyboard, to type, lightning speed.*

AN ABSOLUTELY AMAZING ORGAN

The brain consists of grey and white matter. It weighs just over a kilo, but this is a very special kilo. It uses twenty percent of the body's energy. And it contains over one hundred billion cells. These make up neurons, or nerve cells, which are connected by electrical impulses. The brain sends messages using electrical impulses, the same way a computer works. But there are more possible connections in one brain than there are atoms in the universe. Amazing! This makes a normal computer look simple.

Neuroscientists, scientists who study the brain and the nervous system, have learnt a lot about it in recent decades. Like explorers exploring the world, they have mapped different areas of the brain which are responsible for different functions. We now know which parts of the brain are related to different parts of our body and feelings from them. A good example of this can be seen in people who have lost an arm or a leg in an accident. Though they don't have an arm or a leg they can still have feelings from it, like pain.

Specific areas of our brain control all our movements. To put up an arm, for instance, electronic impulses need to be sent to the arm from the brain. It is really quite a complicated operation. The areas of the brain related to controlling sight and hearing could be compared to miniature film studios which make a constant film and soundtrack of what is happening around us. It is not our ears that listen, but our brains. It is not our eyes that see, but our brains. Our eyes and ears send signals all the time, and it is our brain that interprets these signals and builds up a picture of the outside world... Of course, there are other areas of the brain that scientists have identified, areas responsible for different emotions – for fear, for love, for laughter. There are different areas for different kinds of thinking – there is one area for our first language, and another one for a foreign language that we learn...

----

matter
Matter is physical substance; food is matter whereas love is an emotion.
weigh
Put the load on the weighing machine!
Some fruits are sold by weight, others by number.

percent
We are expecting a 30 per cent increase in the prices of meat.
What per cent of the population attend / attends private schools?
Only a small percentage of students failed.
universe
Universe is, in fact, the (whole) combination of all matter, energy and space.
Astronomers are learning more about the universe.
English is becoming a universal language spoken on all continents.
map
He drew a rough map to show us how to get to her house.
The area has not yet been mapped.
movements
The dog watched my every movement.
The dentist asked her not to move her head.
operation
Do you understand the operation of a car engine?
Can he operate the machinery you have here?
He is a computer operator.
studio
Studio is the workroom of an artist, photographer, etc.
The TV comedy show is recorded before a live studio audience.
signals
The signal coming in from the damaged ship was very weak.
The policeman signalled to the driver to pull over.
The heavy rains signalled the end of the drought.
interpret
It is not always easy to interpret a symbolic painting.
The actor gave a new interpretation of the part of Hamlet.
build up
It took years of hard work for him to build up the business.
The doctor found a build-up of fluid in her knee.
You must not drive at speed in a built-up area.
identify
Can you identify this butterfly?
Please give us proof of identity when you pay by cheque.
Shops demand some form of identification when you pay by cheque.
connections
Make this connection/connexion *watertight*.

- **Can you tell the difference between *interpret* and *translate*? Give some examples of your own using:** *trek, track, soundtrack, watertight, water proof, bullet-proof.*

A bit too hot, I'm afraid!

New reports being published all the time confirm global climate change. For the last three decades temperatures have been above average and the temperature has risen steadily since 1910, owing to the increased burning of fossil fuels and emissions of carbon dioxide – the famous 'greenhouse effect'. The increase in the twentieth century was only 0.6° C, but this has actually meant major changes in climate. North America has regularly had temperatures 3° C higher than usual and both the Arctic and Antarctic ice caps are melting. The latest computer forecasts predict that global warming could speed up and meteorologists predict an increase of 6° C in the twenty-first century. This will have unforeseen consequences for the future.

Recently released statistics also show the number of endangered species on the 'red list', that is species on the brink of extinction. This list has grown dramatically in the last few years. Over a quarter of the world's reptiles and a fifth of the world's amphibians are all threatened by the destruction of their habitats. Eleven species of mammals are in danger and these include tigers, whose population is down to 5,000, and giant pandas, whose population is around 1,000 owing to deforestation. However, there is some good news. The white rhino, which in 1970 was on the verge of extinction with only 200 animals left, has now recovered, and there are now 11,000 white rhinos in the wild.

Recent population figures suggest that the world's growth is beginning to slow down. World population has doubled since 1960 and is over six billion. Growth has mainly been in the developing world. In many African countries well over forty percent of the population is under fifteen, whereas in the developed world this figure is under twenty percent. Despite this, some experts suggest that the world population will have stabilised at around nine billion in the year 2070. Unfortunately, the important thing to point out is that the number of *poor* people in the world is actually increasing. Poor people make up one third (!) of the world's population. And that's despite a steady increase in global income since 1960. Basically, the world has got richer, but the number of poor people is going up! And what is worrying, too, is that the gap between rich and poor is growing as never before.

----

average

To pass, students must average 50% throughout the year.

We have had above / below average rainfall this month.

fossil fuels

Coal is fossilised/fossilized wood from the remains of the pre-historic forests.

Coal and oil are fossil fuels which will be used up one day.

emission

The explosion was caused by an emission of gas from a leaking valve.

carbon dioxide

Plants give off the gas carbon dioxide.

He made a carbon copy of that important document.

greenhouse effect

A greenhouse is used for rearing plants under controlled conditions.

Global warming may result from the greenhouse effect.

melt

The melting point of a metal is very high.

The alloy is prepared in a melting pot.

forecast

The sales forecast for next year shows an upward trend.

To forecast means to estimate or calculate what is likely to happen.

brink of extinction

She stood on the brink, wondering if the water was cold.

He was on the brink of a new career when he fell seriously ill.

amphibians

An amphibian hatches larvae that live in water.

The soldiers used an amphibious landing craft.

destruction

The hurricane caused much destruction on the island.

A destroyer is heavily armed and highly manoeuvrable.

deforestation

Deforestation has caused havoc to the ecosystem in certain parts of the world.

slow down

Please slow down, you're talking too fast!

stabilise

This old chair isn't very stable.

A stabiliser is a device that makes something steady, stable.

make up

Water is made up of two parts hydrogen to one part oxygen.

It is not in his make-up to cheat.

gap

This new product should fill a gap in the market.

She took a computer course to fill the gap between school and university.

- **Can you give your own definitions/explanations of:** *fuel, emission, reptiles, programme, brink, verge, havoc?*

LANDMARKS OF SCIENCE IN THE 20th CENTURY

In the summer of 1905, a young man was sitting at home after a day's work. While rocking his one-year-old baby, he thought something over. Suddenly, it came to him! The famous equation $e = mc^2$ was born, an equation which would change our understanding of the universe but would help to create the nuclear bomb. Albert Einstein was aware of recent developments, such as Marie Curie's research into radioactivity, but he had been working on his own. His mould-breaking equation showed how a small piece of mass could produce an unbelievable amount of energy. Einstein then demonstrated in his 'theory of relativity' that not even time, mass or length are constant – they vary according to our perspective of them. For example, if we could see people moving at the speed of light, they would appear much heavier and larger and would seem to move in slow motion.

By the time Einstein had become world-famous, a young ex-lawyer returning from the First World War started work at the Mount Wilson Observatory in California. Using the most high-powered telescope of its time, he began a painstakingly slow observation of nebulae, small patches of light that appeared outside our galaxy. Edwin Hubble was on the brink of making the greatest astronomical breakthrough of the century. He discovered that these nebulae were in fact galaxies like our own, millions of light years away from us, which proved that the universe was vastly larger than had previously been thought. Then, Hubble proved that the universe is actually expanding and that the further away galaxies are the faster they move.

During the Second World War the US Navy were looking for ways of improving the accuracy of their artillery shells, but this involved incredibly complex calculations. The navy turned to Eckert, an engineer, and Mauchly, a physicist to produce a machine to do the job. Although they and their team did not finish the machine until after the war, in February 1946, it did not matter. They had produced the world's first computer. ENIAC (Electronic Numerical Integrator and Computer) was huge, measuring 100 feet long by over 10 feet high and weighing over 30 tons. It contained 18,000 tubes and had more than 6,000 switches. It was extremely difficult to program. The ENIAC project failed to meet its original objective, but it certainly gave the world its first computer.

----

science
Physical sciences include physics and chemistry.
Science requires theories to be tested and proven.
equation
It is a mistake to equate wealth and happiness.
2y + 5 = 11 is an equation.
nuclear bomb
When a nucleus splits, nuclear fission occurs.
A nuclear bomb was dropped on Hiroshima in World War II.
mould
Molten gold is poured into moulds.
At the factory, steel is moulded into rods.
mass
A mass of spectators waited to see the film star.
constant
You must keep these chemicals at a constant temperature.
vary
He has tried many jobs in a varied career.
The pupils copied the diagram with varying degrees of accuracy.
There are usually various ways of solving a problem.
observatory
They gathered in the observatory to observe and record the eclipse of the sun.
telescope
The Hubble space telescope revealed more details on that nebula.
nebulae
The future may reveal even more distant nebulae/nebulas.
galaxy
A galaxy may extend over thousands of light years of space.
Galactic travel is the theme of many science-fiction films.
expand
Metals expand when heated and contract as they cool down.
Could you expand on your plan and give us some more details?
accuracy
Use an accurate scale to measure these ingredients.
The accuracy of that old clock is amazing.
shell
Shells are designed to explode in the air or upon impact.
The artillery will shell the enemy positions.
tubes
The tube had to be replaced when our old television broke down.
switches
Where is the switch for the lights?
He switched the train onto the other track.

- **Now you make sentences with:** *landmark, inequation, light years, expansion, artillery, bomb, bombard, integrate, integrator, objective.*

To remember about Mathematics...

The first thing to remember about mathematics is that it is not simply a matter of writing down numerals, x's and y's; it is more a way of thinking. Playing a game of cards is, of course, using mathematics, but you do not call it by that name. You know elementary mathematics all right, but you have not learned the language. And you are not going to get far with the study of Homer until you have familiarized yourself with the Greek alphabet.

Have you ever paused to consider the really quite difficult mathematical procedures you are using every day without realizing it? Think of the knowledge (though it be unconscious knowledge) of geometry that is required for a game of billiards. Or of the complicated calculations and estimates needed to hit an archery target. You must judge the size and distance of the target, the weight of the arrow as against the estimated velocity, and you must allow for cross-current of air. Even if you could feed all this data into a computer it would do you little good; some of the conditions would have changed by the time you had lodged your information. Again, a rifle-shooting competitor allows for wind and estimates the drop in the parabolic curve that the path of his bullet will take as the result of gravity, although he does not call himself a mathematician and probably could not tell you what a parabola is.

You have obviously from time to time crossed the road, and clearly the amount of mathematical calculations you have done (even though you may not be aware of it) might give pause to a Newton. You have estimated the speed of the cars approaching from both directions as well as your own speed (allowing, let us hope, a margin for safety) and you have decided the most direct route you can take while avoiding the traffic. Apart from using the estimates correctly, you will have used geometry, trigonometry and the calculus, even though you may deny even a nodding acquaintance with any of these subjects. And yet you accomplish this feat daily with repeated success! It is because each one of us has tucked away in his skull a built-in computer. And it is a very reliable instrument indeed. It is as good (though of course not as fast) a computer as the latest model on the market; that is to say, it will never make a mistake unless you feed it the wrong information.

----

numerals
This computer program uses an alphanumeric / alphameric code.
pause
He spoke excitedly, without pausing.
The hikers paused at the top of the hill.
procedures
The procedure for opening a bank account has been simplified.
geometry
In geometry we learn that the angles in a triangle add up to 180°.
A geometry set includes a set square, pairs of dividers and compasses, a protractor, ruler, etc.
calculations
We use a calculator to work out the answer.
She made an error in the calculation.
estimates
I estimate it will take a month to complete this job.
archery; arrow
An archer is a person who shoots with a bow and arrow.
The archer's arrow hit the bull's-eye of the target.
This arrow shows the way to the exit.
velocity
The velocity of a bullet decreases because of air resistance.
gravity
Things fall to the ground because of gravity.
Spacecraft must achieve great acceleration to escape the Earth's gravitational pull.
ordeal
Being lost in the mountains was a frightening ordeal for her.
speed
The car accelerated and gathered speed.
Mercury was the speedy messenger of the gods.
The driver was travelling at speed and couldn't brake in time.
route
The quickest sea route from Europe to Asia is via the Suez Canal.
The plane was routed to Tokyo via Hong Kong.
traffic
Air traffic increases at high season.
The traffic lights turned red, bringing the traffic to a standstill.
trigonometry
Trigonometry is often shortened to *trig*.
Trigonometry is the branch of mathematics dealing with relationships between the sides and angles of triangles.
tuck away
Their holiday house is tucked away behind a hill.

* **Try now to make sentences with:** *alphabet, account, unconscious, cross-current, feed data into, lodge, parabolic curve / parabola, margin, calculus.*

Deadly Nuclear Waste Under Rec Center?

In the late 1970s, UCLA professor Dan Hirsch heard from some of his students that the future site of the Barrington Recreation Center in the tony LA suburb of Brentwood was sitting atop a dark secret. There was talk that Veteran Administration doctors and staff had been quietly dumping nuclear waste from the hospital into a landfill for almost twenty years.

Hirsch formed a coalition of his students to look into the charges and soon found that the rumors were true. They uncovered a paper trail indicating that the hospital had indeed used the area as a dump for waste from the radiation therapy program, and perhaps even from a small reactor. "The main concern here is that the radiation could have gotten into the soil, which in turn would have been absorbed into the vegetation. Remember, this stuff sticks around for years, hundreds of years," Hirsch is quoted as saying in the book *L.A. Exposed*, by Paul Young.

What Hirsch and his students didn't count on was a confrontation with a Brentwood lobby group, who insisted that soccer and baseball fields be built on the radioactive real estate. These people, wealthy parents of local kids, didn't believe the stories about the nuclear waste, perhaps thinking that some developer had planted them to scare away the competition.

The Nuclear Regulatory Commission (NRC) was called in to investigate. After a perfunctory sweep of the area with a Geiger counter, the NRC pronounced the area safe. Not satisfied, Hirsch was able to secure an LAPD helicopter to fly him over the property with an infrared camera, which might reveal radioactive 'hot spots'. However, on the appointed day, he arrived to find that someone had gone over the area with a bulldozer, wiping out any vegetation that would show up hot on the infrared pictures. Hirsch was later told that the timing of the plowing was merely a coincidence! If the waste is buried more than a few feet underground, the radiation should be well contained and the NRC can be trusted in this case, even though it didn't take the simple and obvious step of obtaining soil samples

----

nuclear waste
Nuclear waste is the waste material from creating nuclear power.
They have enough bombs to *nuke* us all one day.

Veteran Administration
In North America, an ex-soldier is often called a vet.
This tournament is for veteran golfers exclusively.
He was appointed administrator of the fund.
The administration of justice is not easy.
dump
Dump that load of gravel over there!
The refuse / rubbish was discarded on the town dump.
landfill
The town's landfill site is quickly being used up.
coalition
We hope that those two sections will coalesce into a single department.
charges
Shoplifting is a chargeable offence.
radiation therapy
Radiation therapy is the treatment of disease by radiation, especially X-rays.
Cancer patients receive radiotherapy.
absorb
He is absorbed in his game of chess.
There is rapid absorption of moisture by plants in hot weather.
confrontation
The boxers confronted each other in the ring.
You must confront your problems, not avoid them.
lobby group
We should lobby officials to devote more money to training.
The lobbyist rallied public opinion against whaling.
real estate
A *realtor* is an accredited real estate agent.
developer
Many people live in this new housing development.
I know the property developer well.
perfunctory sweep
Unmotivated students do their homework in a perfunctory manner.
The busy teller served me perfunctorily.
Geiger counter
Geiger counter is an instrument used to detect and measure radio-activity.
infrared; infrared camera
The infrared band lies between visible light and microwaves in the electromagnetic spectrum.
bulldozer
They used a bulldozer to demolish the cottage.
The boss bulldozed the plan through the meeting.
plowing/ploughing
The ploughshare is the sharp metal blade of the plo**ugh**/plo**w**.

- **Can you explain the meaning of:** *UCLA, LAPD, rec center, rumo(u)rs, Nuclear Regulatory Commission, reveal, lobby, samples?*

Santa Cruz Mystery Spot

There is a place in California where the laws of physics do not seem to apply. Here water flows skyward and people can actually walk up walls. American mystery spots, like the one located in Santa Cruz, are a time-honored classic among roadside tourist traps. With wild claims of antigravity vortices and dizzying sensations, how could these places fail to entice the curious? Are they merely off-kilter rooms designed by highway hucksters to disorient the hapless tourist? Or are they really places that belie all that science has taught us about the way the universe operates?

Visitors to the college town of Santa Cruz have often observed how ... odd the local culture seems to be. They note the town's many peculiar characters, its eccentric civic politics, its vast array of bohemian subcultures, and – more darkly – its onetime status as the mass-murder capital of the world. And they wonder what makes this attractive beach town seem even more bent than its sister university city, Berkeley, fifty miles to the north, several times larger, and far more famous as a counterculture weirdness-incubator.

The answer might lie in a hundred-fifty-foot-wide patch of land just north of the city called the Mystery Spot. First discovered in 1939 and opened to the public a year later, this hillside lot is one of North America's most famous and visited 'vortices' – sections of land where the laws of gravity, perspective, and even physics are suspended.

Originally, the land around the spot was slated to be a summer-cabin site. When surveyors attempted to chart the lot, goes the story, they found that their instruments would not give accurate readings over one particular piece of land. People who visited this spot claimed that a force seemed to be trying to push them off-balance, making them light-headed and dizzy. Recognizing a good thing when they saw it, the owners opened up the site as a tourist attraction, claiming that strange forces were at play on the hill.

----

physics
Physics is the science of matter, forces and energy.
A nuclear physicist helped to design the nuclear power station.
Physical chemistry is the use of physics in the study of chemistry.

apply
Applied maths is used in engineering.
The rule applies to all members.
vortices/vortexes
The diver was sucked down into a vortex.
entice
Enticing smells came from the kitchen.
Ads are designed to entice people into buying things.
hapless
Hapless is an old-fashioned word for unlucky, or wretched.
belie
Her cheerful words belie her grief.
amble
To amble means to walk at an unhurried pace
shrouded
The town was shrouded in mist.
The company operated in a shroud od secrecy.
array
There was an impressive array of vintage cars at the motor show.
mile
What is the mil(e)age between your home and the office?
He's miles better at tennis than I am.
incubator
The plan had been incubating in his mind for some days.
The eggs were hatched by artificial incubation.
perspective
From that hill you get a perspective of the entire valley.
This perceptive writer puts the war in historical perspective.
suspend
This car's excellent suspension gives a smooth ride.
You should suspend judg(e)ment until you know all the facts.
slate
Slate is a dark grey rock that splits easily into flat layers.
I put my keys in the fridge, *I must have a slate loose* (slang expression for *I must be crazy*)!
chart
Your job will be to chart the progress of the project from start to finish.
The navigator plotted the ship's course on the chart.
lot
Excuse me, where's the nearest parking lot?
readings
The thermometer reads 30°C in the shade.
The electricity meter should be read every month.

- **You should now give your own examples using:** *admission, shroud, hucksters, redwood, vintage cars, suspension, fridge, parking lot.*

The Moonraker

It was like being inside the polished barrel of a huge gun. From the floor, forty feet below, rose circular walls of polished metal near the top of which he and Drax clung like two flies. Up through the centre of the shaft, which was about thirty feet wide, soared a pencil of glistening chromium.

The shimmering projectile rested on a blunt cone of latticed steel which rose from the floor between the tips of three severely back-swept delta fins that looked as sharp as surgeons' scalpels. But otherwise nothing marred the silken sheen of the fifty feet of polished chrome steel except the spidery fingers of two light gantries which stood out from the walls. Where they touched the rocket, small access doors stood open in the steel skin and, as Bond looked down, a man crawled out of one door on to the narrow platform of the gantry and closed the door behind him with a gloved hand. He walked gingerly along the narrow bridge to the wall and turned a handle. There was a sharp whine of machinery and the gantry took its padded hand off the rocket and held it poised in the air like the forelegs of a praying mantis. The whine altered to a deeper tone and the gantry slowly telescoped in on itself. Then it reached out again and seized the rocket ten feet lower down. Its operator crawled out along its arm and opened another small access door and disappeared inside.

"Probably checking the fuel-feed from the after tanks," said Drax. "Gravity feed. Ticky bit of design. What do you think of her?" He looked with pleasure at Bond's rapt expression.

"One of the most beautiful things I've ever seen," said Bond. It was easy to talk. There was hardly a sound in the great steel shaft and the voices of the men clustered below under the tail of the rocket were no more than a murmur.

Drax pointed upwards. "Warhead," he explained.

----

cling
Wet clothes cling to the body.
Die-hards cling to their old-fashioned beliefs.
shaft
A golf-club shaft is precision made.
The mine shaft was closed by a rock fall.

soar
New York is full of soaring skyscrapers.
Soaring prices and wages cause spiralling inflation.
shimmer
Shimmer is a soft, flickering light.
The waves shimmered in the moonlight.
projectile
The latest field guns can project shells for many kilometres.
A rocket is a projectile.
blunt
This pair of scissors is too blunt to cut the material.
Too little sleep can blunt a driver's reactions.
cone
Orange traffic cones signify that road works are in progress.
The witch in the fairy tale wore a conical hat.
The police have coned off one lane of the freeway.
delta fins
An aircraft with a swept-back, delta wing has a triangular appearance.
scalpel
Scalpel is a surgical knife.
The surgeon made a cut with her scalpel.
sheen
Sheen is a bright surface, glass or lustre.
Newly washed hair in good condition has a natural sheen.
gantry
Gantry is a frame that acts as a support – for a crane, or road signs, for example.
A space rocket is supported by a gantry before launching.
whine
The saw makes a terrible whine when it cuts metal.
telescope in
This little umbrella folds up telescopically.
In the accident the car was telescoped.
crawl
There's a beetle crawling across the floor.
The traffic was reduced to a crawl owing to the road works.
gravity feed
Things fall to the ground because of gravity.
rapt expression
She was so rapt in her book that she didn't hear the doorbell.
warhead
Warhead is the explosive head of a weapon/missile.

- **Try to make some sentences of your own, using***: fashion, fashionable, old-fashioned, modern, skyscraper, corrosion, foam-rubber, access doors, handle, fuel-feed.*

ELECTROMAGNETIC WAVES

Electromagnetic waves come from a number of sources and are the effect of oscillating electric and magnetic fields. The wavelength of these waves varies but all travel through free space (a vacuum) at approximately 300,000 kilometres per second, which is the speed of light. The *electromagnetic spectrum* contains waves from low frequency/long wavelength radio waves (long wave) through microwave, infrared and the visible spectrum to ultraviolet X-rays and the short wavelength/high frequency gamma rays.

Electromagnetic waves are generated when particles with an electrical charge change their energy, e.g. when an electron changes orbit around a nucleus. It also happens when electrons or nuclei oscillate and their kinetic energy changes. A large change in energy produces high frequency/short wavelength radiation.

Radio waves are the longest in the spectrum and are used to transmit sound and pictures. *Microwaves* have wavelengths of a few centimetres and have numerous uses. *Infrared* (IR) waves are generated by the continuous motion of molecules in materials, and hot objects give out most. When an electric fire is switched on the infrared radiation is felt in the heat. As objects become hotter and hotter, their molecules vibrate more rapidly and the wavelength of the radiation becomes shorter. Eventually it impinges on the visible spectrum and the object appears 'red-hot'. *Ultraviolet* (UV) radiation occurs beyond the violet end of the visible light spectrum, is a component of sunlight and is emitted by white-hot objects. Ultraviolet light from the sun converts steroids in the skin to essential vitamin D but an excess of UV light can be harmful. However, much of the sun's ultraviolet radiation is stopped by the Earth's ozone layer. *Gamma rays* are very short wavelength radiation released during radioactive decay and are the most penetrating of all radiations.

----

wavelength
The wavelength of a radio signal determins its frequency.
We get on well because we are on the same wavelength.
vary
He has tried many jobs in a varied career.
Prices are subject to variation without notice.
vacuum
A flame cannot burn in a vacuum.
Vacuum is a space from which all air or matter has been extracted.

electromagnetic spectrum
Our school includes pupils with a wide spectrum of abilities.
A spectrometer can measure the wavelength, energy and intensity of a spectrum.
spectre – The old castle had a gloomy, spectral atmosphere.
ultraviolet
The ultraviolet rays of the sun cause tanning and skin cancer.
particles
There wasn't a particle of doubt about his guilt.
electrical charge
That drill is electrically powered.
The atmosphere was charged with emotion.
This flat battery needs to be charged.
orbit
The sun appeared like a fiery orb on the horizon.
The Queen carried an orb at her coronation.
This is outside the orbit of my responsibility.
nucleus
When a nucleus splits, nuclear fission occurs.
oscillate
The pendulum will oscillate if the clock is wound.
kinetic energy
Kinetics is the study of bodies in motion.
molecules
Each molecule is made up of two or more atoms.
vibrate
The guitar string vibrated when she plucked it.
impinge
Impinge is a formal word meaning to have an effect on.
white-hot objects
The filament of a light bulb glows white-hot.
In the white heat of battle, the soldier hardly felt his wounds.
essential vitamin D
Essential oils are used in massage and aromatherapy.
ozone; ozone layer
Ozone is used in bleaching, sterilizing water, and purifying air.
Ozone depletion is caused by polluting the atmosphere.
radioactive decay
The Roman Empire fell into decay.
Regular brushing with toothpaste should prevent tooth decay.
penetrating
Sound can not penetrate these thick walls.
No-one can fully penetrate another's mind.
That brilliant scholar has a penetrating mind.

- **It should not be difficult now to make some sentences using:** *oscillating fields, gamma rays, pluck, light bulb, purify, brush, ozone depletion.*

DESKTOP PUBLISHING

DTP (*desktop publishing*) is the software and hardware that make possible the composition of text and graphics as would normally have been done by a printer or in a newspaper office. Desktop publishing requires the use of a computer, laser printer, and various software programs to prepare and print documents. It is possible to produce anything from a single page of text to advertisements, pamphlets, books and magazines. Computer-aided publishing has been possible since the early 1970s for organisations willing to invest large sums of money, e.g. traditional printers or publishing houses. Desktop publishing as a function of personal computers (PCs) became possible on a broad scale only in 1985, with the introduction of the first relatively inexpensive laser print producing 'letter quality' type and visuals.

A basic desktop publishing system allows its printer to produce print by employing a variety of fonts and type sizes, type justification, hyphenation, and other typesetting capabilities offered by DTP software programs. Page layouts, based on a template, can be set up on the computer monitor and transferred, as seen on the monitor, to the printer. Many types of graphics can be created, and the system may also incorporate art and photographs from sources inside the computer. The command codes for producing text and graphics are comparatively simple. Some computers use symbols and a pointer controlled by the mouse; others use word and letter commands. A basic DTP system includes a microcomputer, a laser printer that is able to print at 300 or more dots per inch (dpi), word processing software and a page description language; a software program that enables its user to position, size, and manipulate blocks of type and pictures.

In contrast to professionally printed matter, 300 dpi provides relatively low resolution. More complex laser printers or the use of an added phototypesetting unit produces finer quality print and illustrations. The addition of a computer-connected scanner allows the use of text and visual material from other sources.

----

newspaper office
News to be broadcast or printed has first to be processed in the newsroom.
desktop publishing
Desktop publishing – DTP – enables us to produce high-quality printed matter with a desktop computer and printer.

laser printer
A laser can cut hard substances such as metals.
My laser printer produces high-quality copy compared to my old dot-matrix printer.

computer-aided publishing
CAP stands for Computer-aided publishing, CAD for Computer-aided design.

fonts
Font is the old-fashioned or poetic word meaning fountain or well.
Font is also a basin in a church, often carved from stone, to hold water for baptisms – a basin for holy water; The proud parents held their baby at the font in the church.
Font / fount is a set of printing type of one style and size.
Each font / fount includes a complete alphabet, numerals and punctuation marks.

type justification
Justify means to adjust lines of typing so that the margins are straight.

hyphenation
Do you hyphenate "boyfriend"?
The hyphen links a compound word like "ex-wife" or divides a word into syllables at the end of a line.

page layout
The company hired a landscaper to lay out the gardens at their new headquarters.

template
A template / templet can be used as a guide for cutting or drilling metal, stone, wood.

incorporate
The Committee will incorporate your evidence in its report.

pointer
A cat's whiskers point outwards.
She asked for some pointers on how to improve her test results.

dots per inch
A dot-matrix printer uses dots to form letters.
Be here on the dot of six o'clock!

resolution
You must show more resoluteness and work harder.
The resolution of this telescope lens is so good that you can see the smallest craters on the moon.

phototypesetting
He writes his stories on a portable typewriter.
Many typists use computers nowadays.

scanner
Ultrasound scanning is used to examine the growing fetus.
The document is scanned by the fax machine before the image is sent down the telephone line.

- **Give your own examples using:** *desktop computer, aid, on a broad scale, punctuation marks, type sizes, craters, typist, typewriter, keyboard.*

NUCLEAR ENERGY

Nuclear energy is the energy produced by the controlled decay of radioactive elements. Upon decay, an element such as uranium releases energy as heat which can be harnessed – the energy given off per atom is thousands and thousands of times more plentiful than during burning.

Nuclear fission is the splitting of such atoms and is the way in which electricity is generated from nuclear power. In a *nuclear reactor* heat from the nuclear reactions heats water into steam, which drives the turbines. The core of a reactor contains the nuclear fuel, which may be uranium dioxide with uranium-235. Neutrons produced by the fission reactions are slowed down by a graphite core to ensure the *chain reaction* continues. A chain reaction develops when the neutrons go on to split further nuclei, and the energy released becomes enormous. The graphite core is called the *moderator*. *Control rods* of boron steel are lowered into or taken out of the ractor to control the rate of fission. Boron absorbs neutrons, and so if rods are lowered there are fewer neutrons available for the nuclear fission, and the reactor core temperature will fall. This is a *thermal reactor*. In a *fast breeder reactor,* low grade uranium surrounds the core, and impact from neutrons creates some uranium-239, which forms plutonium, which itself can be used as a reactor fuel.

Nuclear fusion has not yet been harnessed for commercial power production. It happens when two nuclei are combined to form a single nucleus with an accompanying release of energy. Ordinarily nuclei would repel each other because of the like electrical charge, and so very high collision speeds have to be used, which in practice means the use of incredibly high temperatures. Because thermal energy has to be supplied before the nuclear reactions occur, fusion is often called *thermonuclear fusion*. Fusion occurs in the Sun and, in an uncontrolled way, in the *hydrogen bomb*, but it is technically very difficult to control in the way that nuclear fission is managed.

Nuclear energy has the benefit of producing a lot of energy from a small amount of fuel. It does not produce gases that contribute to the *greenhouse effect*, but the waste produced is very dangerous and must be stored or treated very carefully.

----

controlled
An air-traffic controller monitors aircraft from a radar screen.
The pilot is at the controls in the cockpit.
decay
Vegetation decays (rots away, decomposes) to form *compost.*
harness
The skydiver put on his parachute harness.
We must harness the sun's energy to provide us with heat and power.
nuclear fission
Nuclear fission releases tremendous energy.
electricity
Electrons and protons contain electricity.
The era of steam trains ended when the railways were electrified.
generate
Friction generates heat.
Electricity is generated by a dynamo or generator.
nuclear reactor
A nuclear reaction is a change within the nucleus of an atom.
A nuclear reactor produces nuclear energy.
neutrons
A neutron carries no electricity.
A neutron bomb kills people through radiation but does little damage to buildings.
the rate of sth.
Your rate of progress is to slow.
Prices are increasing at a steady rate.
low grade
Eggs are graded according to size.
The house collapsed because low-grade bricks were used.
A grader is a machine used to level the ground.
repel
Like poles of the magnets will repel each other.
Oil repels water, does not mix with it.
This fabric is water-repellent.
This spray repels flies.
the like electrical charge
We share many interests, we're like minded.
Don't compare a cheap radio to a music system, only compare *like with like.*
You even talk the same way, *like mother – like daughter*!
collision
The radar screen shows two planes on a collision course!
Communism and capitalism have colliding (conflicting, opposing) ideologies.

- **Make sentences of your own using the words and expressions:** *cockpit, compost, uranium, graphite, boron steel, to compare like with like, to have opposing ideologies.*

FACSIMILE TRANSMISSION

A *fax* (short for *facsimile*) *machine* is a device capable of transmitting or receiving an exact copy of a page of printed or pictorial matter over telephone lines in, usually, less than 60 seconds. Facsimile transmission in some form has been available since the end of the 19th century (Alexander Graham Bell invented *telephone* in 1876 and a public service was begun three years later after Bell had brought his invention to the UK) but remained a relatively specialised communications device until the development of sophisticated scanning and digitising techniques in computer and communications technologies, and the establishment of standards that made it possible for all fax machines to communicate with one another over ordinary telephone lines.

Most contemporary fax machines conform to a set of standards, known as Group III, that were implemented in 1980 and require digital image scanning and data compression. Machines built to conform to Group III standards can transmit data at a maximum 9,600 bits per second (bps). To transmit, the original document is fed into the machine, where it is scanned by a mirror- -and-lens-aided device, or, in some faxes, by a series of light-emitting diodes (LEDs). Light and dark picture elements – pixels, or pels – are described digitally, and the message is shortened by compressing much of the white space. The receiving machine, which is addressed through its telephone number, translates the code it receives back into a pattern of greys, blacks and white. The reconstituted message is printed out on heat-sensitive paper, using techniques similar to those for copying machines, office machines for producing duplicates of printed matter. Some fax machines can actually double as copiers, and modern machines use ordinary paper, which eliminates the use of heat-sensitive paper that browns over a period of time.

----

fax / facsimile
A facsimile is an exact copy, accurate reproduction.
A fax (fax machine) makes communication much easier.
I've faxed her a copy of the document.
pictorial
It's a pictorial calendar with a large colour picture for every month.
She gave a pictorial description of that holiday spot in her letter.

telephone
Telephony makes communication quick and simple.
The telephonist will put you through to the right department.
communications
Storms have severed all communications with the town.
The fax is an instant form of written communication.
Measles and chickenpox are highly communicable diseases.
Communications satellites make it easy to relay TV signals all over the world.
sophisticated
Computers are becoming smaller and more sophisticated (advanced, complex).
Living in Paris made me more sophisticated (cultured, refined; fashionable, ...).
digitise; digitising
On digital audio tape, sound is recorded digitally.
establishment
She has established herself as an author of children's books.
Management should establish good relations with its staff.
data compression
The information captured is stored as a database and can be retrieved at any time.
Data processing is the sequence of computer operations that analyse information, solve problems, etc.
Try to compress your lengthy speech into five minutes!
bits per second (bps)
bit is an acronym for *binary digit*.
A bit is either of the two digits (0 and 1 in the binary system) used as units of information in a computer's memory.
pixels / pels
Pixel or pel is an acronym of *picture element*.
A pixel / pel is the smallest unit of colour in a picture on a computer or video screen.
translate the code
I wasn't sure whether to translate (to interpret) his silence as agreement or disapproval.
How will the government translate (transform; express or put in another form) policy into action?
duplicate(s)
Do you have a duplicate key to the safe?
We have to duplicate the document on the copier.
double as
If you double two, you get four.
In that play he doubles as the butler, and the doctor.
We were doubled up with laughter at his jokes.
brown
Leaves turn brown in autumn. They brown.

• **Now you try to make sentences of your own with:** *confidential matters, mirror-and-lens-aided device, light-emitting diodes (LEDs), pattern, retrieve, acronym.*

The rays that penetrate solid matter

X-rays are electromagnetic waves with a short wavelength (approximately $10^{-10} - 10^{-8}$ m) and are produced when electrons moving at high speed strike a target and are stopped very quickly. They were discovered in 1895 by Röntgen. He found that wrapped photographic plates left near a working cathode ray tube became fogged as if they had been exposed to light and he called this unknown radiation X-rays.

Atoms of all elements give out characteristic X-rays when hit by electrons. The stream of electrons colliding with the atom displaces electrons from inner orbitals and vacant places are then filled by electrons from the outer orbital, which give out energy as they move down. X-rays have the properties of electromagnetic radiation and also penetrate solid matter, cause ionisation (by removal of electrons from atoms), make some materials fluoresce and, as mentioned, they affect photographic film. These properties render X-rays both useful and hazarduous. Their ionisation effect damages living tissue, but by using very small doses, they can be used in medicine to take X-ray photographs of the body. The extent to which the rays are absorbed depends upon the density and the atomic weight (or relative atomic mass) of the material; the lower these factors, the more easily will the rays penetrate. The greater density of bone means it is possible to take an X-ray photograph because the flesh appears transparent while the bones are opaque.

X-rays are also used in industry for checking joints in metal and examining flaws. They are also used in *X-ray diffraction* (or X-ray crystallography) which is an analytical tool in geology, crystallography, and biophysics. X-rays directed at the sample are diffracted off the planes of atoms in the crystal. By repeating the procedure and then calculating the spacing between atomic planes, a representation of the crystal's structure can be determined.

----

solid matter
A semiconductor is a solid-state device. (of electronic components, using only transistors not valves)
The milk in the freezer has frozen *solid* (adv.).
A baby has to be gradually introduced to solid food or solids.
Compare the solidity / solidness of this old oak table with that flimsy modern one!

strike sth.
The tree was struck by lightning.
cathode tube, cathode ray tube
Is there anything worth watching on the *tube* (slang for a TV) tonight?
This metal tubing is part of the cooling system of the fridge.
to become fogged
Foglamps help to improve visibility when travelling in mist or fog.
The bathroom mirror has fogged *over/up* because of steam from your hot bath!
stream
Streamlined trains can reach high speeds.
Water streamed from the ruptured pipe.
orbitals
The orbital road (a road circling a city) speeds up traffic on the highway.
The satellite orbited the Earth for ten days.
properties
Many herbs have medicinal properties.
Petrol has the property of removing tar stains.
ionisation
An ion can be positively or negatively charged.
The ionosphere reflects radio waves and makes long-distance radio communications
possible.
fluoresce
The flickering of a faulty tube in the fluorescent lighting at the office has given me a headache.
tissue
The silver jug was wrapped in non-tarnishing tissue paper.
Smoking can damage your lung tissue!
density
The density of the fog made driving impossible.
He is too *dense* (stupid, dull) to understand that joke!
transparent
The transparency of the water lets us see every detail of the lake bottom.
He writes in a transparent style so his meaning is crystal clear.
opaque
The opacity / opaqueness of the water is caused by the soap.
He didn't follow those opaque (difficult to understand) comments.
joints
Cut the stem above the joint of the third leaf!
The whole schedule is out of joint due to the strike.
flaws
His argument is flawed and can easily be disproved.
plane(s)
Graphite has carbon atoms lying in flat planes.

- **You could make some additional examples, using:** *flimsy, opponent, anode, cathode, medicinal properties, medicinal herbs, joints, flat planes.*

Electrons act as minute magnets

Magnetism is the effective force which originates within the Earth and which behaves as if there were a powerful magnet at the centre of the Earth, producing a magnetic field. The magnetic field has its north and south poles pointing approximately to the geographic north and south poles and a compass needle or freely swinging magnet will align itself along the line of the magnetic field. With the correct instrument it can also be seen that the magnetic field dips into the Earth, increasing towards the poles.

A *bar magnet* has a north and a south pole, so named because the pole at that end pointing to the north is called a north-seeking pole, and similarly with the south pole. When dipped in a material that can be magnetised, such as iron filings, the metal grains align themselves along the magnetic field between the poles of the magnet. Some materials can be magnetised in the presence of a magnet, e.g. iron and steel. Iron does not retain its magnetism, but steel does. These are called *temporary* and *permanent magnets*. A more effective way to produce a magnet is to slide a steel bar into a solenoid (coil) through which current is passed and magnetism is *induced* in the steel (*electromagnet*).

In addition to iron, cobalt and nickel can also be magnetised strongly and these materials are called ferro-magnetic. Non-metals and other metals such as copper, seem to be unaffected by magnetism, but very strong magnets do show some effect.

The origin of magnetism is unknown, but is attributed to the flow of electric current. On the electronic scale within magnetic materials it is thought that electrons act as minute magnets (because electrons carry a charge) as they spin around their nuclei in atoms. In some elements, this electron spin is cancelled out but in others it is not and each atom or molecule acts as a magnet contributing to the overall magnetic nature of the material.

----

minute
Read the minutes of the previous meeting, please!
I want it minuted that I disagree with this decision!
The minute steak was served with onions and tomatoes.

compass
Compass is an instrument used for finding directions.
My geometry kit includes a pair of compasses.
That high note is beyond the compass of the singer's voice.
align
The tyres will wear unevenly as the wheels are not in alignment.
The candidate is an independent, not aligned with any political party.
dip into
He had to dip into (to draw upon) his savings to buy new furniture.
People dip into magazines in doctors' waiting rooms.
pole
These calculations are all up the pole (slang for difficulty or error).
The Pole Star was formerly used as a guide for sailors.
The negative and positive poles of a magnet attract each other.
iron filings
A file can be a steel hand tool with small cutting teeth.
Sweep the filings ((metal) particles removed with a file) away!
To file means to smooth or shape with sth. that is rough-surfaced.
retain
Sponges retain water.
This retaining wall will hold back the flood waters.
The way he retains facts makes him a walking encyclop(a)edia.
slide
She slid into the room unnoticed.
Property values are beginning to *slide* (fall gradually).
Weeks of heavy rain caused a mud slide down the mountain.
nickel
Nickel is used in alloys, in electroplating, and so on.
The letters EPNS on cutlery stand for electroplated nickel silver.
A *nickel* in Canada and the USA is worth five cents.
The ornament has a nickelled finish.
origin
There are many theories about the origin of life on earth.
She is the originator of this plan.
He comes from poor, working-class origins.
spin
Spin a coin to decide who will begin!
He spun the roulette wheel.
Her head was spinning from turning round and round.
The tennis player put so much spin on the ball that her opponent misjudged it.
cancel out
This good fortune has cancelled out (made up for) all my past troubles.

- **Can you make sentences of your own, explaining the meanings of:** *policy of non-alignment, solenoid, cobalt, nickel, a nickel, a dime, ferro-magnetic materials, misjudge?*

Machines and Mechanics

Machine is basically a means of overcoming resistance at a point by applying a *force* at another point. Although a machine does not reduce the amount of work to be done to achieve a task, it does allow a work to be done more conveniently.

There are six *simple machines* in the study of physics. These are the *wheel* and *axle, wedge, lever, pulley, screw,* and the *inclined plane.* Each in its own way can be used for a particular task – the lever or pulley to raise a load, the wheel to transport a load, and so on. More complex machines usually involve the input of energy either for modification or for driving a mechanism to achieve a task.

The *mechanical advantage* of a machine is the ratio of the load moved to the effort put in to achieve the movement. The *velocity ratio* is the distance moved by the effort divided by the distance moved by the load. An inclined plane, or *ramp,* does not appear very much like a machine but it is because it enables a load to be taken gradually to a height to which the load could not have been lifted vertically. In this case the velocity ratio is essentially the length of the ramp over the height of the ramp.

Mechanics is the part of physics that deals with the way matter behaves under the influence of *forces.* It involves: *dynamics*, which is the study of objects that are subjected to forces that result in changes of motion; *statics*, which is the study of objects subjected to forces but where no motion is produced; *kinematics*, which is the study of motion without reference to mass or force but which deals with velocity and acceleration of parts of a moving system.

Newton's law of motion forms the basics of mechanics, except at the atomic level, when behaviour is explained by *quantum mechanics.*

----

mechanics
A mechanician / mechanist is a person skilled in making machinery or tools.
The pumping mechanism of our washing machine needs fixing.
resistance
He has a stubborn resistance to becoming computer literate.
This paint is rust-resistant.
The urge to laugh was irresistible.

achieve sth.
To achieve means to accomplish something successfully.
Winning that match was an achievement.
Winning tomorrow's match is an achievable goal for us, believe me!
axle
An axle is the rod on which a wheel turns.
We seem to have broken the back axle of the car.
wedge
Put a wooden wedge under the door to keep it open.
Cut a wedge of cheese from the big round.
Split the log by putting a wedge in the crack and hammering it in.
lever pulley
Manual drive cars have gear levers.
His political connections are a lever to make business contacts.
The engine drives this car's cooling system by means of a pulley.
screw
The handle is attached to the door with four screws.
Screw the lightbulb into the socket!
She screwed her head around to look behind her.
Use a flat screwdriver as a lever to open this lid!
inclined plane / ramp
Ramp is a slope or incline, usually joining two different levels.
We climb down the ramp (a movable set of steps) when leaving an aircraft.
The handle is attached to the door with four screws.
A ball will roll down an inclined surface.
He has an inclination for scientific subjects.
I am inclined to daydream during boring lectures.
velocity
The velocity of a bullet decreases because of air resistance.
the basics of sth.
You will be able to buy all the basics (necessities) at that shop.
He has a basic (vulgar) sense of humour that sometimes offends people.
We meet on a regular basis.
behaviour
We are studying the behaviour of lions in their natural habitat.
We expect you to be on your best behaviour in church!
quantum mechanics
Quantum mechanics or quantum theory is a theory to describe how electrons, protons and neutrons make up atomic molecules (atoms).

- **You should try now to explain the meanings of:** *literate, computer literate, illiterate, crack, hammer, air resistance, offend, habitat.*

Driver & Application Installation

Step 1:
Turn on your PC and start up the Windows.
Step 2:
Shortly after entering the Windows, you will see the **Found New Hardware Wizard** dialog box. Click *Cancel*.
Step 3:
Insert the Multimedia Software CD into your CD-ROM drive. Autorun will start and the menu screen will appear. Click the button marked *WinFast TV Capture Card* on the virtual remote control.
Step 4:
Choose the language for the installation. Click *Next*.
Step 5:
The driver installation is going to start. Click *Next*.
Step 6:
The wizard is installing the driver. A window will appear indicating the status. Please wait.
Step 7:
If warning messages show up, please click *Continue Anyway*.
Step 8:
The installation is finished. Please choose *Yes, I want to restart my computer now* to reboot your computer, and click *OK*.
Step 9:
After reboot, the wizard will automatically install WinFast application. Please choose the language for installation and click *Next*.
Step 10:
A dialogue box will appear telling you the installation of WinFast PVR2 application is going to start. Click *Next*.
Step 11:
Please click *Yes* in the next few steps to continue.
Step 12:
Please click *OK* to finish the entire installation.

----

installation
An electrician is to insta(l)l new wiring in our old house.
The installation of air conditioning cost more than expected.
She installed herself in my favourite armchair.
The enemy installation is vulnerable to attack.

driver application

A driver is a device that transports data to or from a disk.

Steam drives the engine, it keeps machinery going.

application

Use this applicator to spread the glue.

This new device has several applications in industry.

Applied maths is used in engineering.

You will never be promoted if you don't apply yourself to your work.

It's a complicated job that requires great application (hard work or effort).

click

The door closed with a click of the latch.

She clicked her tongue disapprovingly.

It finally clicked where I had met him before.

We clicked (became friendly; took a liking to each other) from the moment we met.

remote control

Many TV sets allow you to switch channels by remote control.

They live on a farm remote (adj.) from any town or village.

In the remote past, dinosaurs roamed the Earth.

I haven't the remotest idea on what this foreigner is saying!

He doesn't even remotely resemble his father.

wizard

Wizard is a male witch who practises witchcraft or magic, a sorcerer.

He used his wizardry to mix a magic potion.

A wizard is also somebody who is exceptionally good at something, a genius.

She's a wizard at languages.

warning (messages)

"Beware of the dog", the sign warned.

She glanced at him warningly.

reboot / restart

To reboot means to shut down and then restart.

I had to reboot the computer to get it functioning properly again.

entire

That glutton ate the entire (whole, complete) cake.

She is entirely blameless.

We must examine the problem in its entirety!

guide

Sailors used to be guided by the stars.

Be guided by your conscience!

The aircraft was downed by a surface-to-air guided missile.

- **Try to make sentences illustrating different meanings of:** *air conditioning, vulnerable, latch, resemble, conscience, conscientious.*

The ozone layer

The ozone layer is between 15 and 40 kilometres up in the atmosphere, higher than most aeroplanes fly. This region contains most of the atmosphere's ozone, which is a special form of the gas oxygen. Ozone has the unique ability to stop certain dangerous invisible rays from the sun from reaching the Earth's surface – rather like a pair of sunglasses filters out bright sunlight. These rays are known as ultra-violet radiation. This damages living cells, causing sunburn and more serious diseases. The ozone layer is vital to life on the surface of the Earth.

Until the ozone layer formed, about two thousand million years ago, it was impossible for any living thing to survive on the surface of the planet. All life was deep in the oceans. But once oxygen was formed in the air, and some of that oxygen turned to ozone, plants and animals could begin to move on to land.

Humans, however, are now damaging the ozone layer for the first time. In the past couple of decades, scientists have discovered that some man-made gases, used in everything from refrigerators and aerosols to fire extinguishers, are floating up into the ozone layer and destroying the ozone. The most common of these gases are called chlorofluorocarbons – CFCs.

The damage is worst over Antarctica, and near the North Pole, where scientists have seen small holes appear for a short time each spring since 1989. So far, those holes have healed up again within a few weeks by natural processes in the atmosphere that create more ozone. But each year, it seems to take longer for the healing to be completed. Also, all round the planet, there now seems to be less ozone in the ozone layer than even a few years ago. The problem is that it takes roughly eight years for CFCs, which are released when an old fridge is broken up, to reach the ozone layer!

----

layer
After the bush fire a fine layer of ash covered everything in the house.
Layer chocolate sponge and cream to make a delicious cake!
atmosphere
Atmospheric conditions influence the weather.
Atmosphere refers to the gases that surround the Earth or any celestial body.

filter out
News of his promotion filtered *out/through* to his colleagues.
You must filter the water to remove impurities.
vital (to life)
The heartbeat and breathing are two of the vital signs of human life.
She is a vital person full of high spirits.
Her vital statistics (a woman's bust, waist ahd hip measurements) are 92, 71, 97 cm.
survive
The cattle cannot survive the drought.
Are there any surviving stars of silent films?
The dead woman is survived by her two children.
These special forces are taught survival skills.
Winning this game is vital if we are to stay in the tournament!
humans
The humanities include literature, languages, history and philospohy.
Nuclear warfare could wipe out humankind.
Children's cartoons humanize animals by making them talk.
It is not humanly possible to live in water.
aerosols
Do you use an aerosol deodorant or a roll-on?
Spray the insecticide aerosol to get rid of the cockroaches!
fire extinguishers
I keep an extinguisher in my car in case of fire.
Poor eyesight extinguished his ambition to be a pilot.
float up
Cork floats supported the fishing net in the water.
Has anyone seen my keys floating about?
Because of their buoyancy, wood and cork float on water.
heal up
Look how the horse's hoof had healed up nicely!
Put a healing lotion on the burn!
She prefers to go to a *faith healer* rather than a doctor.
fridge
Butter and milk should be kept in a fridge to prolong their freshness.

- **In sentences of your own, illustrate the meanings of***: celestial bodies, sunbum, strong spirits, drought, silent films, tournament, a roll-on, insecticides, extinguish, chlorofluorocarbons, fridge.*

NAVIGATION

In ancient times the navigation of a vessel depended on the experience of the master. Gradually various aids were added to help the captain in this responsible work. For many centuries seamen had to rely on a knowledge of the coasts and basic astronomy and it was a long time before they left the coastal waters and ventured out on to the open sea. Thus proper sea voyages began only in Viking times, around AD 1000. Then came the discovery of the compass and hour glasses, and the use of the astrolabe, cross staff, log and finally the sextant, all of which were crucial to the voyages of discovery. In addition to written navigation instructions, which seem to have been possessed by early sailors, imperfect maps were in use at the dawn of the New Age.

Techniques developed in the eighteenth and nineteenth centuries provided for near-perfect navigation, even on long ocean voyages, though risks continued to be great. Even today when excellent navigation aids supply the master with continuous bearings giving his ship's geographical position, data of speed, depth, exact time and meteorological and radar information, collisions still occur, fires break out, ships run aground and sinkings cause loss of human life and valuable cargo. It is indeed surprising how many ships are lost every year, despite perfect communication between bridge and engine room by means of telegraph, telephone and the automatic transmission of orders and data; despite the ever increasing perfection of steering and navigation equipment, such as gyropilots, radars, radiolocators and remote-control systems; despite perfect radio and telegraphic communication, despite the safety and watch services at sea, excellent maps and charts, lighthouses, radio sending stations, lightships, and coastguard signals. The causes of such losses include derelictions of duty by officers and crew, imperfect design and construction of a vessel or mistaken evaluation of communications data; and the unpredictable power of the sea and nature, which man has tried to master for over a thousand years of sailing history.

----

navigation
Pilots use modern navigational aids to stay on course.
That hopeless navigator can't follow a map.
vessel
Vessel is a formal word for a ship or boat.
Veins and arteries are blood vessels.

venture out
Explorers venture forth on hazardous journeys.
No-one ventured to argue with the boss.
voyage
Voyage is a long journey, especially by sea or air or through space.
Yuri Gagarin was the first voyager in space.
hour glasses
Use this small hourglass to time the boiled eggs.
astrolabe
astro- is a prefix meaning *of the stars, of outer space.*
The astronomer sighted a new comet.
Computers have speeded up astronomic(al) calculations.
log
The pilot had logged 300 hours flying time on jets.
sextant
A sextant can be used to measure the angles of the stars or sun to fix a ship's position.
crucial
Getting this job is crucial (decisive) to my career.
bearings
Check the compass bearing to see whether we are heading the right way!
Get the map out, we will need to find our bearings before we go any further!
What you said has no bearing on the problem.
run aground
Unfortunately, the ship ran aground (touched the bottom in shallow water) during the storm.
cargo
The ship carried a cargo of wheat.
bridge
Bridge is a raised platform on a ship from which it is piloted and navigated.
The new bridge is a triumph of engineering.
steering equipment
Hold the steering wheel with both hands!
The steersman guided the boat into the harbour.
They travelled *steerage* (the cheapest accommodation on a passenger ship) to Australia.
Steer clear of (avoid) that troublemaker!
gyropilots
The model globe will gyrate around its axis when you spin it.
radiolocators
The pilot radioed the airport for help.
The pilot adjusted his course to the next radio beacon.
derelictions
The old ship is now in a state of dereliction (deserted, forsaken, left to fall into ruins).
He was sacked for dereliction of duty (neglect of responsibilities).
Don't trip over the derelict (a social outcast, vagrant) sleeping on the pavement!

- **Make sentences of your own, explaining the meanings of:** *ancient, to rely on/upon sbd., astronomy, hazarduous, gyrate, lightships, outcast, outlaw.*

The Martians Are Coming!

What I marvel at now, when I remember the days when the Martians were speeding earthward, is our unconcern. The catastrophic Things were hurtling on, and lovers wandered through English lanes with no thought of the danger above their heads.

Late that afternoon I saw the Martian. When the lid fell off from the hot cylinder that was like a meteorite, something like a snake wriggled into sight. I stood stricken with terror. A round body, about four feet across, pulled itself painfully to the opening.

I had expected to see a man, fantastic, perhaps, but two-legged. This thing was just oily, leathery body, legless, and armless, with a chinless and noseless face. Two great eyes, dark and luminous, were mirrors for an extraordinary brain. Evolution had made them all brain, cold, remorseless intelligences unswayed by emotion.

The creature panted and heaved. An intense loathing came over me. I ran madly.

"Way! Way!" The Martians are coming!

"Ellen!" shrieked a woman in the crowd, with tears in her voice. "Ellen!" And the child suddenly started crying: "Mother!" trying to reach her in the terrified crowd.

"They are coming", said a man on horseback.

"I can't go on! I can't go on!" a little man was weeping.

"Out of the way, there!"

I stumbled on, panic-stricken. The monsters could slay with heat rays beyond the range of our biggest guns. Terror stalked through London. To the horror of heat rays had been added the black smoke, a cloud of poison that blighted all living things. So London streamed in flight, 6,000,000 people roaring out along highways until they were like rivers in flood.

The metropolis was stilled out of all its humming life.

----

speeding; earthward
I remember the days when the Martians were speeding earthward.
wander
Lovers *wandered* in the parks with no thought of (the) danger.
cylinder
The hot cylinder was like a meteorite.
Cylinder is a solid or hollow object with circular ends and straight sides.
meteorite
A meteorite is a meteor which is large enough to reach the Earth's surface.
strike
A devastating earthquake struck Japan.
She was struck dumb with astonishment.
I stood there, stricken with terror.
legless, armless, chinless; remorseless
They were cold, remorseless intelligences unswayed by emotion.
stumble
We stumbled about in the dark.
range
The aircraft came within our range of vision.
guns
Revolvers, pistols, rifles and cannons are all types of guns.
blight
Illness has blighted her career.
roar
Trucks roared past us on the highway.
humming (adj.)
There was silence except for the hum of traffic in the distance.

- **Give your own examples with:** *wriggle, shriek, heat rays, extraordinary.*

David the teenage tycoon

Teenager David Bolton has just put £9,000 in the bank – after only six months of part-time work as a computer consultant. The electronics expert from Croydon, South London, is fast establishing a reputation as one of the country's top troubleshooters – the person to call if no one else can cope.

For David, 15, his first steps to fame and fortune began when he was only nine, when his parents bought him a computer, a ZX-90. 'I soon learned to program it. I needed something bigger, so I had to save for ages to buy an Amstrad.'

It was only about a year before these words, however, that he had decided to get serious about computing. He went to night school to learn how to write business programs, and did a correspondence course with an American college.

He got in touch with a computer seller, Eltec, who were so impressed they gave him computers and software worth more than £3,000. In return, he has to send them a monthly report saying what he has done and what his plans are. He helps companies by suggesting which computers they should buy, and by writing individual programs for them. He can work more quickly than many older professionals. In one case, he went to a company where a professional programmer had worked for six months and could not find the problem. David finished the job in five days.

It is because of work of this standard that in the short period he has been in business David has made about £9,000. With it he has bought more equipment. How did he do it? 'You have to be ambitious, and you have to really want to get to the top. Believe in yourself, and tell yourself that you're the best.'

----

tycoon
That tycoon owns a number of publishing houses.
consultant
A public-relations consultant can help you to improve the image of your company.
expert
Ask him about your problem, he's a computer expert.

cope
She is coping well, despite all her problems.
Can you cope with this extra work?
to program a computer
Can you program this computer to check my spelling?
correspondence course; to do a course with
He has enrolled with a correspondence college for a correspondence course in marketing.
seller
How much does the seller want for his car?
software
He loaded the software to play a computer game.
Keyboards, monitors and printers are all computer *hardware*.
programmer
My brother is a computer programmer.
equipment
Computers are standard office equipment today.

* **Make your own sentences using***: part-time work, troubleshooter, to get to the top, to put a sum in the bank.*

Something Out of Star Wars?

Has the sun turned green? Not exactly. That glowing blob was actually a solar flare that hurtled toward the Earth in mid April, 1997, and was caught on camera by NASA's SOHO spacecraft. The sun spat out the flare – it is actually tons of charged hydrogen and helium, same as the sun – and propelled it toward Earth at about 2.4 million kph. Flares normally occur every three or four years, stretch across 50 million km and take anywhere from 16 hours to several days to pass Earth. This one was the largest since a 1989 flare that knocked out a power grid in Quebec for nine hours.

Flares can disturb the Earth's magnetic field and give heart attacks to electric wiring, telephone lines and electronic transmissions. Earthlings need not fear. Scientists say that such flares are harmless to humans, and the few common effects are limited to missed telephone calls and TV programs. "Maybe people will read again," mused a flare-watcher in New York. Another perk: flares set off pretty auroras such as the Northern Lights.

----

to turn green
He turned his loss into profit by improving sales.
Her health took a turn for the worse.
flare
The match flared and then burnt steadily.
The lifeboats are equipped with flares that can be fired into the air in an emergency.
My bad knee has flared up again.
spacecraft
A spaceship is a manned spacecraft.

spit/spat out
He tends to spit when he talks quickly.
Burning logs sometimes spit out sparks.
propel
The rowing boat is propelled by oars.
Space rockets use either a liquid or solid propellant/propellent.
knock out
To knock out means in fact to eliminate.
They were knocked out in the third round of the tournament.
His wife is gorgeous, a real *knockout* (slang for an extremely attractive person).
power grid
A grid is any network of lines, pipes, etc.
A grid of freeways crisscrosses Los Angeles.
magnetic field
A magnetic field is the area where a magnetic force of attraction is exerted.
Earthlings
Earthlings are human beings, especially in science fiction.
In the book I'm reading, earthlings were captured by aliens from outer space.
muse (v.)
To muse ≈ to ponder; Teenagers often muse over their future.
"What should I do now?" – he mused.
perk
Perk usually appears as a shortened form of perquisite.
Political power was once the perquisite of the upper classes.
aurora; Northern Lights
Aurora ≈ *aurora borealis* is the term for bands of mainly red and green lights
seen in the sky at night near the North Pole.
The Northern lights are probably electromagnetic in origin in the ionosphere.

- **Now you try to give your own examples using**: *star wars, blob, solar flare, hurtle, charged hydrogen, helium, kph, electronic transmissions.*

Arctic obsession remains relevant

Adventure, failure and disaster in one of the most hostile environments on Earth are the subjects tackled in an exhibition at the National Maritime Museum in London. *North-West Passage: An Arctic Obsession* features more than 120 objects ranging from maps, letters, drawings and paintings to native Inuit artefacts from 19th century with the aim of bringing British exploration of the Arctic to life.

The exhibition concentrates on the many failed and disastrous expeditions undertaken by explorers keen to discover and map the passage, which they believed would act as a lucrative trade route between Europe and the East. However, the exhibition is not just a nostalgic stroll through history, but is intended to raise environmental and political issues in the minds of visitors as well.

Spokesman for the museum Nigel Rubenstein, said: – The exhibition is certainly motivated by environmental issues. The Catlin Arctic Survey is currently measuring the thickness of the ice in the region, as well as the current impact we are having on the region's wildlife. This and current issues of sovereignty, due to the oil deposits in the area, mean this exhibition is about both the modern and the historical. The whole world is once again focussing on the Arctic region.

Some of the key artefacts on display include relics recovered from Sir John Franklin's doomed voyage in 1845, which offer a stark illustration of Arctic survival techniques. Also on show will be drawings from John Ross' 1829 voyage, which document the first encounter with the native Inuits as well as the original flag staff used to mark the discovery of the magnetic north pole in 1831.

----

obsession
He is obsessed with the fear of growing old.
She is obsessive about punctuality.
disaster
Disaster is an event that causes great damage or harm.
The flooded town was declared a disaster area.
That play was a total disaster (fiasco, failure).

hostile
The more conservative workers are hostile to any change.
Animals have adapted to survive in the hostile environment of the Sahara Desert.
Inuit
Inuit / Innuit / Innuits are aboriginal peoples of North America, formerly called Eskimos.
lucrative
Hiring videos used to be a lucrative business until a couple of years ago.
Look at all this lovely lucre we've won!
stroll
Tourists stroll along the beach.
We were strolling along, window-shopping.
impact
Impact is a collision between two bodies; a violent encounter.
Torpedoes are designed to explode on impact.
The Industrial Revolution had a huge impact on the world.
wildlife
There are bear, deer, and other wildlife in these hills.
The injured falcon was treated and then released back into the wild.
sovereignty
The military raid into the neighbouring country was a violation of its sovereignty.
A sovereign (a former British gold coin) was originally worth one pound sterling.
oil deposits
There are many oilfields in the Middle East.
Oil wells are characterized by tall structures which drill for, and pump, the oil out of the ground.
focus (v.)
If you focus the sun's rays through a magnifying glass onto dry grass, it will start burning.
She focuses on a problem with real determination.
The crash focused/focussed attention on safety.
Try focusing/focussing on one job and getting it done before moving on to the next!
relics
Stone-age relics were found at the archaeological site.
Many relics are displayed in museums.
stark illustration
The stark truth is that we can't afford a new car.
The stark (bare, harsh, simple) desert landscape was unbroken by vegetation.
staff
A staff is a strong stick used as a support, weapon or symbol.
Staff is also a set of five horizontal lines on which music is written.

- **Now try to give your examples using:** *adventure, failure, environment, expedition, explorers, modem/fashionable.*

Who exactly are the poor people of the world?

Some social groups are much more likely to be poor than others. If you are a woman, if you come from a group of the original inhabitants of a country, like the Native Americans in America or the Aborigines in Australia, if you are old, or if you are a refugee – you are much more likely to be poor than other people.

The big question we need to answer is: why does poverty exist? Why are some countries so much poorer than others? There are many possible causes of poverty. A country may be poor simply owing to its location. Areas with poor soil and bad climates are more likely to be poor than others. Related to this is the environment. Poor countries are usually the ones that suffer from natural disasters, such as hurricanes and floods. There are also historical reasons for poverty. Some countries, particularly in Europe and North America, experienced industrial development in the past, and industrial growth made them richer. Many other countries did not develop industrially. In fact, they were often exploited by the industrial nations and remained poor. These countries had to borrow from the developed countries and still owe huge amounts of money in foreign debt. One final cause of poverty is politics. Countries which are unstable politically, especially those which have suffered war or civil war, tend to be poorer.

Here it is worth mentioning the poverty trap, what we might call the 'vicious circle' of poverty. This is very important at a personal level. Many poor children in the world have to work to help their families. This means that they do not get a good education. Because they do not have educational qualifications, they can only get the worst jobs. These jobs pay low wages, and so they have little money to bring up their children. Now their children have to go to work and so *their* education suffers – and so the vicious circle continues.

So what can be done about poverty? In 1996, the United Nations asked the world's richest countries to put aside 0.7 percent of their GNP (gross national product) for aid to developing countries. In the meantime, only a few countries met that target and some even cut down on aid programmes!

Native Americans
The terms American Indian, or Amerindian or Amerind are all used to describe the indigenous American people.
Kangaroos are native to Australia.
Aborigines
The aborigines were originally nomadic hunters.
He collects aboriginal weapons from Africa.
cause
Dirt is the cause of (the) infection.
Constant, causeless anxiety will affect your health!
location
In the geography exam we had to locate four towns on a map.
We must find a suitable location for a camp.
climate
Latitude, altitude and proximity to a coast contribute to the climatic conditions of an area.
A knowledge of climatology is essential for weather forecasting.
environment
How can you concentrate in such a noisy environment?
We need laws to prevent further pollution of the environment.
During my stay I got to know Paris and its environs.
flood
You'll flood the engine with petrol if you keep pumping the accelerator.
Sunlight flooded into the room.
These cheap cameras have flooded the market.
exploit
We should exploit solar energy more as a source of power.
Such a low wage is unfair exploitation.
borrow
To borrow means to obtain something on loan, credit or trust.
Could you lend me your pencil, I'll only borrow it for a minute?
That essay you wrote was borrowed (plagiarized) from a famous author.
trap
Traffic officers trap speeding motorists.
Trap is a device for catching animals or insects.
wages
My mother is the sole wage earner in our family.
The factory workers are paid weekly wages.
GNP
A country's GNP is its gross domestic product plus the total of net income from abroad.
meet the target
The archer was delighted when he hit the bull's-eye on the target.
Advertisers must know their target market.

- **Your turn now! Give examples using:** *refugee, poverty, soil, politics, policy, vicious circle, qualifications.*

Singing Sands and Booming Dunes

Some of the more curious ancient features of the California environment are unquestionably natural, yet somehow this does not diminish their mystery or allure. Take for example sand dunes that sing, stones that race across the parched desert floor in some time-warped game, and briny waves that can be made to sound like the beating of distant drums. While these may all be natural occurrences of the California landscape, because of the strange sensations they evoke in those who experience them, we can perhaps refer to these environmental anomalies as 'unnatural wonders'.

Only seven places in the continental United States are permanent home to the singing-sand concerts, and one of these is in the Mojave Desert on the way to Vegas. Two others are in the far reaches of Death Valley National Park. All the locations have been closed to dune buggies and other assorted sports for many years. The only way in is to hike.

For plain old sand to emit unearthly sounds, the scientists tell us that several exacting factors need to be present: the grains have to be round and between 0.1 and 0.5 millimeters in diameter, the sand has to contain silica, and a certain stable humidity must be present, typically less than 0.1 percent, depending on the size of the grains. The farther the material has travelled to its present home, the better, since as a result of wind and buffeting action against the ground and other sand grains, the individual grains are usually more uniform.

Kelso Dunes, about thirty miles south of Baker, is perhaps the quintessential singing-sand hangout, certainly in California and possibly in the world. The landscape is typical SoCal desert, with Joshua trees and the usual scrub stretching to the horizon. The main sand hill, six hundred and fifty feet high, is visible from the road and is a strenuous hike from the last turnaround. There are a few methods to get the sand to perform, but probably the best instruction would be – Go to the top of the dune and kick sand down the steep side. Make sure the day is calm, since wind will not only mask the sounds, but also tends to make for unstable conditions that keep the sand from cascading evenly. Just walking along the crest of the highest dunes will elicit a sound not unlike a tuba, making each step a musical experience!

----

boom
We could hear the boom of the surf against the cliffs.
allure
The allure of the island was in its isolation.
diminish
If you turn the knob to the left, the sound will diminish.
She is always trying to diminish my achievements!
time warp
His view of life has been warped by his unhappy childhood.
This warped timber is useless for building.
briny waves
Olives are usually pickled in brine (salty water).
dune buggies
There must be a bug in the program causing this error.
hike (v.)
A hiker must wear tough but comfortable shoes.
The hikers climbed slowly up the steep hill.
grains
Grains are any tiny particles.
This photograph is too grainy because it has been enlarged too much.
silica
A computer contains silicon chips.
humidity
It is not so much the heat as the humidity that causes discomfort.
hangout
Where does he hang out these days?
The disco is their favourite hang-out every night.
SoCal
SoCal stands for Southern California.
scrub
The vegetation in this area is mainly scrub.
She scrubbed the wood floor with a scrubbing brush.
horizon
Horizon is the line in the distance where the earth or sea and sky seem to meet.
turnaround
The ship turnround / turnaround time depends on the cargo that is being carried.
cascade (v.)
Thousands of little stars cascade from the fireworks.
A cascade of water tumbled down the rocks.
crest
The boat skimmed the crest of the waves.
elicit
Elicit is a formal word meaning to draw out, or to evoke.

- **It should not be too difficult now to give own examples with:** *desert floor, parched desert floor, wonder* (n.), *Joshua trees, methods, tuba.*

So hang on tight, folks!

As always at the beginning of a flight, Senior Stewardess Gwen Meighen experienced a sense of relief as the forward cabin door slammed closed and, a few moments later, the aircraft began moving. ... *'On behalf of Captain Demerest and your crew ... our most sincere wish that your flight will be pleasant and relaxing ... shortly we shall have the pleasure of serving ... if there is anything we can do to make your flight more enjoyable ...'* Gwen wondered sometimes when airlines would realize that most passengers found such announcements, at the beginning and end of every flight, a boring intrusion. More essential were the announcements about emergency exits, oxygen masks, and ditching. With two of the other stewardesses demonstrating, she accomplished them quickly.

They were still taxiing, Gwen observed – tonight more slowly than usual, taking longer to reach their takeoff runway. No doubt the reason was traffic and the storm. From outside she could hear an occasional splatter of wind-driven snow on windows and fuselage.

There was one more announcement to be made – that which aircrews liked least. It was required before takeoffs at Lincoln International, New York, Boston, Cleveland, San Francisco, and other airports with residential areas nearby.

'Shortly after takeoff you will notice a marked decrease in engine noise, due to a reduction in power. This is perfectly normal and is done as a courtesy to those who live near the airport and in the direct flight path.'

The second statement was a lie. The power reduction was neither normal nor desirable. The truth was: it was a concession – some said a mere public relations gesture – involving risk to aircraft safety and human life. Pilots fought noise abatement power restrictions bitterly. Many pilots, at risk of their careers, refused to observe them.

Now the aircraft had stopped. From a window Gwen could see the lights of another aircraft ahead, several others in line behind. The one ahead was turning on to a runway; Flight Two would be next. Gwen pulled down a folding seat and strapped herself in. The other girls had found seats elsewhere.

----

hang on

Hang on to your old car until you get a better price for it!

The line is engaged, so would you please like to hang on or call later?

cabin

The cabin steward served drinks.

For the cruise, we would like a two-berth cabin.

The hikers sheltered in a log cabin during the storm.

aircraft

Compound words with *air*.

That airliner travels faster than the speed of sound.

The aircraft made an emergency landing.

intrusion

The intrusive noise of aircraft kept us awake.

Don't intrude upon our discussion!

ditch

Water flowed into the irrigation ditch from the well.

I heard she ditched her boyfriend (slang for: to abandon, to leave in the lurch)!

taxi (v.)

Pilots taxi their aircraft to the runway.

The plane is taxiing / taxying towards the airport buildings.

take off

Our flight took off half an hour late.

That was a perfect takeoff by the trainee pilot.

If you're so tired, take yourself off (go away) to bed!

takeoff runway

The plane taxied to the beginning of the runway and then gathered speed for takeoff.

Some fashion models prefer the runway to outdoor shoots.

fuselage

Fuselage is the main body of an aircraft.

The wings of the plane are attached to the fuselage.

residential area

Commuters live in residential suburbs which surround most large cities.

They have emigrated to Canada and taken up residence there.

concession

I must concede that you are right!

The company was obliged to make some concessions to its workers in order to avoid a strike.

abatement

Abate means to become less strong.

The storm will soon abate.

strap (in)

Strap the luggage to the roof rack!

Her strappy sandals had multicoloured straps.

- **You are expected now to give your own examples using:** *stewardess, wonder* (n., v.), *airline, aircrew, fold, folding seat.*

The secret of Doctor No

The two men didn't talk to each other. There was no nervous chatter about how clever they had been, about their destination, about how tired they were. They just drove the machine quietly, efficiently along, finishing their competent job.

Bond still had no idea what this contraption was. Under the black and gold paint and the rest of the fancy dress it was some sort of a tractor, but of a kind he had never seen or heard of. The wheels, with their vast smooth rubber tyres, were nearly twice as tall as himself. He had seen no trade name on the tyres, it had been too dark, but they were certainly either solid or filled with porous rubber. At the rear there had been a small trailing wheel for stability. An iron fin, painted black and gold, had been added to help the dragon effect. The high mudguards had been extended into short backswept wings. A long metal dragon's head had been added to the front of the radiator and the headlamps had been given black centres to make 'eyes'. That was all there was to it, except that the cabin had been covered with an armoured dome and the flame-thrower added. It was, as Bond had thought, a tractor dressed up to frighten and burn – though why it had a flame-thrower instead of a machine gun he couldn't imagine. It was clearly the only sort of vehicle that could travel the island. Its huge wide wheels would ride over mangrove and swamp and across the shallow lake. It would negotiate the rough coral uplands and, since its threat would be at night, the heat in the iron cabin would remain at least tolerable.

Bond was impressed. He was always impressed by professionalism. Doctor No was obviously a man who took immense pains. Soon Bond would be meeting him. Soon he would be up against the secret of Doctor No. And then what? Bond smiled grimly to himself. He wouldn't be allowed to get away with his knowledge. He would certainly be killed unless he could escape or talk his way out. And what about the girl? Could Bond prove her innocence and have her spared? Conceivably, but she would never be let off the island. She would have to stay there for the rest of her life, as the mistress or wife of one of the men, or Doctor No himself if she appealed to him.

----

contraption
What is the purpose of this strange contraption in your garage?
tractor
A traction engine powered by steam or diesel can haul heavy loads over rough ground.
The car skidded because the bald tyres had no traction.
tyres
Her bicycle has a punctured tyre.
trade name
Toyota is a trade name and Tercel is a trademark.
The ingredients of Coca Cola are a trade secret.
solid
Water is liquid but becomes solid when it freezes.
A three dimensional figure (body) in geometry is considered a solid *(n.)*.
porous rubber
Perspiration comes out through the pores of the skin.
A porous sponge will soak up liquid.
trailing wheel
The jet left a vapour trail in the sky.
The car was pulling a boat on a trailer.
iron fin
I saw the dorsal fin of a shark leaving through the water.
Fins stabilize a falling bomb or a rocket in flight.
mudguards
The mudguard protects the bicycle rider from dirt thrown up by the wheel.
radiator
Spokes radiate from the hub of the wheel.
The motorist filled his radiator with water.
headlamps
We could see the headlight of the train in the dark.
armoured
An armoured car gives protection from bullets.
dome
Dome is a rounded roof with a circular base.
The bald professor had a domed forehead.
flame-thrower
His face flamed with embarrassment.
machine gun
Machine gun is an automatic gun that fires continuously.
swamp
Swamp is an area of waterlogged land.
A large wave swamped the canoe.
negotiate
The river is negotiable at only one crossing point.
'Not negotiable' cheques can not be exchanged for cash.

- **Make sentences of your own using:** *chatter, covered, uplands, immense, innocent, innocence.*

Italy hit by quake terror

At least 91 people were killed and 1,500 injured on Monday, April 6, 2009 in Italy's deadliest earthquake for almost three decades. Most were asleep as the 6.3-magnitude quake destroyed 26 towns and villages in just a few seconds, early in the morning. – I woke up hearing what sounded like a bomb – said Angela Plumba, who lives in the mountain city of L'Aquila. – Everything was shaking, furniture falling.

Prime minister Silvio Berlusconi declared a state of emergency as it became clear at least 50,000 people had been left homeless. Another 100,000 fled the quake-hit zone, officials said. L'Aquila main hospital had to be evacuated as fears mounted it could collapse, while the rescue operation was hampered by blocked roads and unstable bridges. – It's a catastrophe; we will never forget the pain – said a survivor who managed to get to a makeshift relief camp with his family.

The quake hit the central Appennine region of Abruzzo at 3.30am. The epicentre was close to L'Aquila, a city of 70,000 people, but tremors damaged buildings up to 100km (60 miles) away. Towns and villages were left strewn with nibble from collapsed homes, offices and churches. – Some towns in the area have been virtually destroyed in their entirety – said parliamentary speaker Gianfranco Fini.

British expat Matthew Peacock, who lives in the town of Amelia, 50km (30 miles) from L'Aquila, described how even the metre-thick walls of his house shook. – It felt like the house was being shaken from the rooftop; my bed was banging against the wall and you could hear creaking. The shaking went on for 20 seconds or so. The earth really felt like jelly underneath.

World leaders, including US president Barack Obama and Pope Benedict XVI, offered their condolences. The EU offered Italy aid but the country insisted it did not need help. Italy has not been hit by a quake of such force since 1980, when 2,735 people died in the town of Eboli.

----

earthquake
Earthquake is a violent disturbance to the earth's surface.
Her resignation will cause an earthquake in that department.

shake
She gave the rug a good shake/shaking to get rid of the dust.
The terrified girl was shaking like a leaf.

a state of emergency
Emergency is a sudden unexpected crisis requiring immediate action.
A state of emergency is declared usually because of civil unrest or a natural disaster.

collapse
That fragile chair may collapse under his weight.
The economic collapse left many without jobs.
We collapsed with laughter at his joke.

rescue operation
Helicopters are ideal for rescuing people from awkward places.
She thanked her rescuer profusely for his help.

hamper
Hamper means to impede; hinder.
Rain will hamper the runners and slow them down.

makeshift
Makeshift is a temporary arrangement, expedient, etc.
This makeshift repair won't last long.

epicentre
Epicentre is the point at which earthquake reaches the Earth's surface.
That troublemaker always seems to be at the epicentre of fights.

tremors
She felt a tremor (a slight trembling or quivering) of fear at the thought of her first flight.

strewn
Strew means to scatter loosely, or sprinkle.
The floor was strewn with her discarded clothes.

nibble
Nibble is a small or gentle bite.
The angler felt a nibble on his line.
In humorous computer jargon a nibble is half a byte or four bits of information.

expat
Expatriate is a person living outside his/her own country.
She is an expat from Serbia now living in America.

creaking
Creak is a harsh squeaking or grating sound.
Creaking doors are used in many horror films.

condolences
We condole with you on your tragic loss.
I must write a letter of condolence to my recently widowed friend.

- **Try to give examples of your own, using**: *quake, decade, zone, catastrophe, Prime Minister, evacuate, parliamentary speaker, underneath.*

Around the world in 46 days ... by albatross

It is a majestic creature which has been part of maritime mythology for centuries. And its movements have always been shrouded in mystery. But scientists have made a remarkable discovery about the mighty albatross – it can fly around the world in just 46 days!

Until now little has been known about what the world's largest bird got up to when it wasn't busy breeding. However, a study has revealed that it likes incredibly long journeys. More than half of the birds studied by a team from the British Antarctic Survey completed a round-the-world trip between breeding seasons. One managed the 13,750-mile journey in just 46 days while three birds circumnavigated the globe twice.

The researchers hope their findings will help reduce the unnecessary slaying of the birds. An estimated 300,000 die each year after becoming caught on fishing hooks. The study, published in the journal *Science*, is the first to show where grey-headed albatrosses go during the 18 months between breeding seasons. Scientists attached tracking devices to the legs of 22 albatrosses.

An albatross will typically spend at least 85 per cent of its life at sea. They are expert gliders – and can sleep while cruising at 25mph. They often look like they are crying because their beaks have tubes that strain out excessive salt from water. Of the 20 different species, the wandering albatross has the widest wingspan: 11ft 6ins. Records have shown albatrosses can live to 80 – but on average it is about 35. Before pairing and mating, they groan, scrape their bills and dance around awkwardly. Their name dates back to the 15th century and is a corruption of ***alcatraz*** – the Portuguese word for *large seabird*.

----

majestic
We saw the Alps in all their majesty (greatness, grandeur, dignity).
The coronation was a majestic display of pomp and pageantry.
maritime
An island may depend on maritime (having to do with the sea or shipping) trade.
A marine is a soldier trained to fight on land or at sea.
mythology
That culture has its own myth about the origins of life.
A dragon is a mythical creature.
The mythology of ancient Greece has tales about their gods and goddesses.

***be shrouded* in**
The town was shrouded in mist.
Clouds shroud the summit of the mountain.
breeding
Swamps provide a breeding ground for mosquitoes.
The French are a breed (a lineage or race) of Europeans.
His perfect manners show his good breeding (social behaviour or background; upbringing).
Some wild animals will not breed (produce young, propagate) in captivity.
circumnavigate
circum- is a prefix from Latin, meaning *around*, *surrounding*, like in: *circumference*, *circumnavigate*, etc.
the globe
That globetrotter has been all over the world.
Magellan was the first to sail right around the globe.
findings
The findings of the Court absolve him of blame.
I saw that money on the floor first, finders keepers.
slaying
Cain slew his brother Abel.
Last night he slayed (slang for impressed, amused, delighted) me with his witty jokes.
When the Mongols captured a town they would slay all the men.
Many soldiers were slain in the battle (a literary word meaning to kill someone violently).
fishing hooks
The angler hooked a big fish.
He thought drugs were harmless but now he is hooked (slang for: addicted to or absorbed by) on heroin.
glider
A glider uses air currents to soar in the sky.
The eagle glided effortlessly through the air.
wingspan
The wingspan / wingspread of a white pelican can be as much as 3 metres.
scrape
Please scrape the mud off your shoes!
Use a scraper to take the old paint off the wall.
The scrape of chalk on a blackboard is annoying.
She only just scraped through the test.
corruption
Weak people are easily corruptible (induced to become dishonest, especially through accepting bribes).
An electronic virus can corrupt (introduce errors into) a computer program.
alcatraz
Alcatraz is the Portuguese word for large seabird.
Alcatraz is escape-proof!

- **Now give your own examples with:** *creature, discovery, journey, research, researchers, beaks, tubes, excessive, species, awkward, awkwardly.*

IZVORI IZ KOJIH SU TEKSTOVI PREUZETI

What Every Pupil Should Know About Physics
The Daily Telegraph Monday November 21, 2005

Our Endangered Planet
Adapted from *Time* Engleski jezik za IV razred gimnazije (Gordana Grba, Karin Radovanović)

Alert over 4 million laptops that could burst into flames
By **Becky Barrow**, Business Correspondent **Daily Mail** Wednesday, August 16, 2006

Branches of Engineering
Adapted from *Engineering English*, by D. Kostić, p. 1

Running scared
Financial Times Tuesday March 4 2008

The Future of Cyberspace
OPPORTUNITIES Pre-Intermediate Students' Book, p. 60

The Laws of Motion and Universal Gravitation
Adapted from *Engineering English*, by D. Kostić, pp. 5-6

Mars, the Red Planet
OPPORTUNITIES Upper Intermediate Teacher's Book, pp. 150-151

Most common problems with radio-controlled vehicles
User Instruction Spring 2007

The Analytical Mind – A Perfect Computer
L. Ron Hubbard, *DIANETICS – The Modern Science of Mental Health* (1986)

How Statistics can fool you
Charles Solomon, *Mathematics* (1969)

A Landmark Science Fiction Film
OPPORTUNITIES Upper Intermediate Teacher's Book, p. 150

What machines can, and can not, do
Charles Solomon, *Mathematics* (1969)

An absolutely amazing organ
OPPORTUNITIES Upper Intermediate Teacher's Book, p. 151

A bit too hot, I'm afraid!
OPPORTUNITIES Upper Intermediate Teacher's Book, pp. 153-154

Landmarks of Science in the 20th century
OPPORTUNITIES Upper Intermediate Students' Book, p.54

To remember about Mathematics...
Charles Solomon, *Mathematics* (1969)

Deadly Nuclear Waste Under Rec Center?
Greg Bishop, *et al.*, *Weird California* (2006)

Santa Cruz Mystery Spot
Greg Bishop, *et al.*, *Weird California* (2006)

The Moonraker
Ian Fleming, *Moonraker*, pp. 84-85 (1974)

Electromagnetic Waves
The Pocket Encyclopedia (2001), pp. 137-138

Desktop Publishing
The Pocket Encyclopedia (2001), pp. 242-243

Nuclear Energy
The Pocket Encyclopedia (2001), pp. 189-190

Facsimile Transmission
The Pocket Encyclopedia (2001), pp. 243-244

The rays that penetrate solid matter
The Pocket Encyclopedia (2001), p. 232

Electrons act as minute magnets
The Pocket Encyclopedia (2001), pp. 178-179

Machines and Mechanics
The Pocket Encyclopedia (2001), pp. 178, 182

Driver & Application Installation
Win Fast TV Series Quick Installation Guide (Spring 2008)

The ozone layer
CAE (2001) Practice Test 4, Paper 1 – Reading

Navigation
SHIPS – A concise guide (1973), pp. 54-55

The Martians Are Coming!
H. G. Wells, *The War of the Worlds* (1898) (adapted)
Engleski jezik za IV razred gimnazije (Gordana Grba, Karin Radovanović)

David the teenage tycoon
HEADWAY Pre-intermediate English Course by John and Liz Soars; Student's book, p. 60

Something out of Star Wars?
By **Amy Wu** *TIME* April 21, 1997

Arctic obsession remains relevant
by Steven Davies *The WHARF*, *wharf.co.uk* May 14 2009

Who exactly are the poor people of the world?
OPPORTUNITIES Upper Intermediate Teacher's Book, p. 154 (adapted)

Singing Sands and Booming Dunes
Greg Bishop, *et al., Weird California* (2006) (adapted)

So hang on tight, folks!
Arthur Hailey, Airport, pp.286-287 (1974) (adapted)

The secret of Doctor No
Ian Fleming, *Doctor No*, pp. 120-121 (1971)

Italy hit by quake terror
by **Aldan Radnedge** *METRO* Tuesday, April 7, 2009

Around the world in 46 days ... by albatross
Daily Mail Friday, January 14, 2005

TESTOVI

Test 1
WHAT EVERY PUPIL SHOULD KNOW ABOUT PHYSICS

1   The atomic ___ says that
all things are made of atoms.

A hypothesize
B hypothesis
C hypotheses
D hyphen

2   The connection between electricity
and magnetism was ___ by Faraday.

A revealed
B relieved
C reveal
D relief

3   Energy can only be ___
from one form to another.

A convert
B converted
C converting
D converter

4   Spontaneous changes are
accompanied by an increase ___ .

A entropy
B tropical
C of entropy
D from entropy

5   Scientists know that
such events are ___ .

A prevention
B preventable
C to prevent
D a prevention

6   Copernicus ___ people that the Earth
was not the centre of the universe.

A convinces
B converted
C conviction
D convinced

7   Can you answer this simple
question: What is ___ ?

A engineers
B engines
C civil engineering
D civilians

8   What are the basic characteristics
of the Industrial ___ ?

A Revolving
B Revolution
C Reveal
D Reformation

9   The book of Nature is written
in the language of ___ .

A mathematician
B mathematical
C mathematics
D mathematician's

10   ___ of energy is not
easy to explain.

A Converter
B Converted
C Convert
D Conversion

11   The discovery of radioactivity
has many practical ___ .

A apply
B application
C applied
D applications

12   Please tell us about Newton's
laws! It is ___ to know that.

A interesting
B interest
C interests
D interested

13   Newton showed us the laws that ___
how things move in the heavens.

A connect
B govern
C convert
D combine

14   The TV is really too noisy!
Please ___ it down!

A put
B turn
C gets
D do

15 Engineering requires above all
the ___ imagination.

A creative
B created
C creates
D creator

16 Our location in the ___
is unlikely to be special.

A universe
B bodies
C building
D universal

17 What do we ___ about the
constitution of matter?

A knew
B feeling
C known
D know

18 Is engineering different
from __ ?

A scientists
B scientist
C science
D scientific

19 Bedrooms all tend
to become __ .

A untidy
B making
C statistics
D station

20 What kind of ___
is called translation?

A motion
B moving
C make
D move

21 Do you know ___ mining and
metallurgical engineering?

A which are
B where are
C which is
D what is

22 ___ must act upon a body
when it accelerates.

A There is
B Force
C A force
D For

23 The Earth's location in the
universe is unlikely to be ___ .

A observation
B inertia
C motion
D special

24 A raised weight can do
___ in falling.

A surface
B smooth surfaces
C working
D work

25 Can we speak about
the ___ of energy?

A creative
B loss
C lost
D last

26 The total amount of energy
___ remains constant.

A universe
B universal
C at the universe
D in the universe

27 Heat is also generated
by ___ .

A nuclear reactions
B reaction
C nucleus
D nuclear

28 The connection between electricity
and ___ was revealed by Faraday.

A magnetic
B magnets
C magnetism
D the magnets

29 The atomic hypothesis says
that all things are made ___ .

A from atom
B of atom
C from atomic
D from atoms

30 ___ is the momentum
of a body?

A What
B Where
C Why
D Your

Test 2
OUR ENDANGERED PLANET

1 ___ organize Earth Day
to dramatize a simple message.

A Environment
B Environmentalists
C Environs
D Environmentalist

2 Our planet is ___ by a number of
man-made ills, e.g. global warming.

A threat
B hypothesis
C threatened
D threatens

3 Scientists are increasingly
concerned about the ozone ___ .

A depletion
B deplete
C converting
D depleting

4 Waste ___ gases are constantly
being discharged into the atmosphere.

A industry
B industries
C industrial
D industrialization

5 Scientists know that such events
are causing ___ change.

A prevention
B climatic
C climatization
D climate

6 Chlorofluorocarbons form
a kind of ___ around the earth.

A blanket
B blank
C blanks
D cylinder

7 Can you answer this simple
question: What is ___ ?

A atmosphere
B atmospheric
C atmosphere's
D an atmosphere of

8 What really happens is popularly
known as the ___ .

A greenhouse
B effect
C greenhouse effect
D green houses

9 The effects of the global warming
___ from place to place.

A very
B vary
C variable
D variety

10 People living in warmer ___
will suffer more severe droughts.

A latitudes
B latitude
C aptitudes
D intelligences

11 Coastal cities might be flooded as
the ice cap melts and ___ sea levels.

A raised
B risen
C rose
D raises

12 Coal, oil, and natural gas
are the so-called ___ fuels.

A range
B fossilized
C fossil
D fossils

13 When such fuels burn,
carbon dioxide ___ .

A is released
B are relieved
C releases
D relieasing

14 We all know chlorofluorocarbons
are not produced ___ .

A natural
B naturalistic
C naturally
D Nature

15 Such gases are widely ___ in
    refrigerators and aerosol sprays.
    A used
    B used to
    C creates
    D uses

16 They are also ___ for the
    depletion of the ozone layer.
    A responding
    B responsible
    C responsibility
    D correspond

17 What do we ___ about the
    depletion of the ozone layer?
    A knew
    B know
    C known
    D tried

18 In what manner are
    chlorofluorocarbons ___ ?
    A destruction
    B destructive
    C science
    D destruct

19 This layer prevents ultraviolet light
    from ___ the earth's surface.
    A reach
    B roared
    C reaching
    D roaring

20 Dangerous ultraviolet light
    increases the risk of ___ cancer.
    A skin
    B skins
    C skinning
    D standing

21 Do you know ___
    acid forests are?
    A which
    B whose
    C what
    D why

22 Our ___ earth faces ecological
    problems of truly global magnitude.
    A danger
    B threaten
    C dangerous
    D threatened

23 The Earth's location in the universe
    is unlikely to be ___ .
    A observation
    B inertia
    C motion
    D special

24 If the problems are man-made,
    they must also be ___ by man.
    A risen
    B solved
    C solution
    D raise

25 The trapped ___ is gradually
    warming the earth's surface.
    A heat
    B energetic
    C hot
    D heating

26 The total ___ of energy in the
    universe remains constant.
    A month
    B amount
    C a month
    D monthly

27 The greenhouse effect is what
    we are increasingly concerned ___ .
    A in
    B of
    C upon
    D about

28 Toxic ___ are one of the
    so-called man-made ills.
    A land
    B lands
    C magnetism
    D landfills

29 These gases ___ the natural
    composition of the atmosphere.
    A alternate
    B heating
    C alter
    D after

30 The title of this text is
    Our ___ Planet.
    A Earth
    B Earth's
    C Danger
    D Endangered

ALERT OVER 4 MILLION LAPTOPS THAT COULD BURST INTO FLAMES

1   The title is: ___ over 4 million
    laptops that could burst into flames.

    A After
    B Aloud
    C Alert
    D Afraid

2   Millions of computer ___ were warned
    yesterday of that potential danger.

    A users
    B used
    C used to
    D user

3   They didn't know that their laptops
    could burst into flames ___ !

    A at moments
    B at any moment
    C moments
    D from that moment

4   That company is the ___
    largest computer firm.

    A world
    B wise
    C world's
    D working

5   Manufacturers hope that such
    events ___ possible in the future.

    A will not be
    B will not
    C were
    D is not

6   The American giant said that
    4.1 million ___ were at risk!

    A machinery
    B machine
    C mechanical
    D machines

7   Some of these batteries
    proved to be really ___ .

    A faulty
    B found
    C fault
    D finally

8   Everything that happened
    came really ___ unexpectedly.

    A quite
    B quiet
    C complete
    D quietly

9   Some other companies ___ now
    whether they could also be affected.

    A interesting
    B investigate
    C interested
    D investing

10 The other ___ computer maker
    does not use such batteries.

    A mayor
    B may
    C might
    D major

11 Photos were presented of a laptop ___
    in the middle of a business meeting.

    A burn
    B inflammation
    C flamed
    D in flames

12 Some customers complain that
    their machines ___ all of a sudden!

    A combustion
    B ignition
    C combustible
    D combusted

13 There are ___ reports of many
    more machines being affected.

    A untidy
    B unconfirmed
    C to confirm
    D understood

14 Can they answer the simple
    question of ___ really happened?

    A who
    B why
    C what
    D which

15 Among owners there were
thousands of British ___ .
A business
B busy
C businesses
D a business

16 The only way to ensure ___ is to
remove the battery.
A safely
B safe
C safety
D saved

17 The customers did not ___ much
about that company's computers.
A knowing
B knew
C know
D knows

18 Owners of such machines
are safe to use them on ___ .
A main
B power
C electrical
D mains power

19 All these batteries carry the
famous manufacturer's ___ .
A brand label
B labelled
C specialized
D brandy

20 These lithium-ion batteries
had to be ___ by the company.
A recalled
B called
C invited
D calling

21 This is believed to be the
biggest ___ of this kind.
A operates
B operation
C operated
D operating

22 Users are, of course, promised
to receive free ___ .
A replacements
B manufactured
C replacement
D produce

23 A laptop was ___ exploding
at a conference in Japan.
A photos
B photograph
C photography
D photographed

24 The problems that were reported
are to be ___ by the manufacturer.
A resolved
B solve
C solution
D risen

25 Manufacturers say they are ready to
continue ___ these serious problems.
A in the spite
B spite
C despite
D in spite

26 One ___ said that the battery produced
explosions for more than five minutes.
A reported
B onlooker
C player
D looking

27 A man was working late in the
office when his laptop ___ fire.
A short
B caught
C has caught
D short-circuit

28 At one moment white smoke
began to ___ of the machine.
A pour
B poor
C pouring out
D pour out

29 This is the fourth problem the firm
has experienced with ___ batteries.
A overheating
B healing
C cool
D harmfully

30 Do you know that lady? She is a
business ___ to the *Daily Mail*.
A correspondent
B editorial
C an editor
D newspapers

Test 4
BRANCHES OF ENGINEERING

1   Can you remember now
    how ___ has been defined?
    A engines
    B engineers
    C engineering
    D machines

2   It is the art of ___ the sources of
    power in nature for the use of man.
    A direction
    B directions
    C direct
    D directing

3   What does the ___ of
    engineering involve?
    A practise
    B practice
    C practically
    D practical

4   In its modern ___ it involves men,
    money, materials, machines, energy.
    A form
    B formula
    C formulation
    D formative

5   It is ___ from science, we must
    bear that in mind.
    A differentiated
    B differ
    C differs
    D difficult

6   Scientists discover and formulate
    the basic natural ___ .
    A phenomenon
    B phenomena
    C phenomenally
    D photos

7   What scientists really do is
    formulate them into ___ theories.
    A accepts
    B accept
    C across
    D acceptable

8   You know this is true,
    historically ___ .
    A speaking
    B talking
    C conversation
    D counting

9   Denis Papin and James Watt are
    the inventors of the ___ engine.
    A steep
    B stem
    C steaming
    D steam

10 This machine first ___ the textile
    trade, that's right.
    A transformation
    B transformed
    C transforming
    D translated

11 It also changed other
    trades and ___ .
    A transporting
    B transportation
    C transit
    D transnational

12 Did you learn about the ___
    Revolution in elementary school?
    A Industries
    B Industry's
    C Internationally
    D Industrial

13 Modern engineering, of course,
    also ___ changes to agriculture.
    A bring
    B brought
    C bought
    D thought

14 Traditionally, there were
    two ___ or disciplines.
    A divide
    B divided
    C division
    D divisions

15 Engineering therefore requires
    above all the ___ imagination.
    A complete
    B created
    C creators
    D creative

16 It is necessary to innovate useful
    ___ to natural phenomena.
    A apply
    B applications
    C appliance
    D applied

17 Engineering is always dissatisfied
    with present methods and ___ .
    A expert
    B equip
    C equipped
    D equipment

18 It seeks newer, cheaper and better
    means of using natural ___ .
    A source
    B sources
    C suffers
    D suppose

19 Energy and materials are used
    ___ man's standard of living.
    A to improve
    B improved
    C reception
    D records

20 It is also necessary
    to ___ laborious toil.
    A defined
    B diminishes
    C destroys
    D diminish

21 Can you tell us something more
    about that ___ engineering?
    A study
    B tradition
    C traditional
    D standards

22 Modern engineering started
    with the ___ of steam engine.
    A invented
    B invent
    C invention
    D prevention

23 These disciplines are military
    engineering and ___ engineering.
    A civilians
    B civilised
    C civil
    D civilisation

24 As time passed, man's knowledge of
    natural phenomena ___ .
    A growth
    B grew
    C grey
    D grow up

25 The potential civil applications
    also became more ___ .
    A complexity
    B complicate
    C compliance
    D complex

26 Civil engineering tended
    to become more and more ___ .
    A specialist
    B specialized
    C specialization
    D speculation

27 The practicing engineers
    began ___ their operations.
    A to restrict
    B restrict
    C restriction
    D restricted

28 The operations were gradually
    restricted into narrower ___ .
    A canals
    B channels
    C tunnel
    D thunders

29 Dams, bridges and buildings
    are the so-called ___ structures.
    A statistics
    B statistically
    C statisticians
    D static

30 Machinery and engines are examples
    of ___ structures.
    A donation
    B dynamics
    C dynamic
    D distributed

Test 5
RUNNING SCARED

1   Bill Gates is a technology
    ___ billionaire.

    A   industry's
    B   industrial
    C   industry
    D   industrious

2   He displays a paranoid tendency
    ___ among such people.

    A   common
    B   communal
    C   coming
    D   commonly

3   You realise you're in trouble
    when it's too late to ___ yourself.

    A   save
    B   said
    C   state
    D   spoke

4   Unless you're running scared
    all the time, you're ___ .

    A   go
    B   gone
    C   went
    D   where

5   Tech fashions and fortunes
    ___ with great speed.

    A   trouble
    B   stay
    C   show
    D   shift

6   *The Microsoft* that Mr. Gates ___
    might not yet belong to history.

    A   hoped
    B   could
    C   founded
    D   found

7   Today even seemingly ___
    companies find it hard to keep pace.

    A   fortune
    B   dominant
    C   dominate
    D   domain

8   *Google* ___ thanks to its obvious
    technological supremacy.

    A   rose
    B   risen
    C   rise
    D   raised

9   The company ___ advertising
    to support the internet services.

    A   used to
    B   used
    C   useful
    D   using

10 *Google* is expected to finally
    ___ the rug from under Microsoft.

    A   push
    B   right
    C   pull
    D   make

11 They will beat their rivals in
    more traditional software ___ .

    A   market
    B   supermarket
    C   marks
    D   markets

12 *Google's* area of ___ is finding
    and manipulating information.

    A   form
    B   focal
    C   formal
    D   focus

13 They manipulate information
    gathered from the world wide ___ .

    A   work
    B   warehouse
    C   factory
    D   web

14 Optimists say that a new ___
    of technology is on the way.

    A   work
    B   where
    C   web
    D   wave

15 It is hard to keep pace in the latest and most promising ___ markets.

A tech
B compute
C businesses
D a computer

16 A decade ago, *Microsoft* was the ___ of the software business.

A leading
B program
C a programme
D leader

17 The company was the feared ___ of that business.

A monopoly
B monopolist
C busy
D manage

18 *Google* also engages in online ___ and advertising.

A computer
B research
C search
D serving

19 *Microsoft* was ___ in advertising by *Google*.

A become
B beat
C busy
D beaten

20 Predicting changes in the tech ___ is almost impossible.

A industrial
B industrialists
C industry
D industrialist

21 *Google's* rise has been a result of its business model ___ .

A innovate
B innovation
C news
D newly

22 It has also been a result of the company's technological ___ .

A supremacy
B supreme
C super
D superior

23 They expect to reach the level of computer-generated ___ .

A reasoning
B reason
C reasonable
D professional

24 It may still take 15 years or more to reach that ___ .

A levels
B solve
C reason
D level

25 Between now and then lies a series of ___ .

A through
B breakthroughs
C thoroughly
D break

26 The way we ___ information from the web will be revolutionised.

A made
B have made
C draw
D break

27 This technology is inspired by AI – artificial ___ .

A intelligence
B intellectual
C intelligent
D intellectuals

28 The question is: How not to be ___ in the end?

A doing
B disappointed
C application
D distribution

29 This technology also uses some of the AI ___ .

A technical
B technician
C techniques
D ambitious

30 Do you understand the title of this text: *Running* ___ ?

A Scared
B Saying
C Scaring
D Soccer

Test 6
THE FUTURE OF CYBERSPACE

1 Computers are certainly going
to __ our lives in the future.

A affect
B effect
C affected
D event

2 We are trying to find ____ how
they are going to change us.

A in
B out
C about
D upon

3 In the last thirty years
the Internet has grown ____ .

A soon
B dramatise
C dramatists
D dramatically

4 In 1983, there were only 200
computers ____ the Internet.

A going
B connected
C connected to
D connection with

5 Now there are over
50 million ____ .

A connection
B confirms
C connections
D confirm

6 We all agree that this ____
is clearly going to continue.

A growth
B grow
C grew
D growing up

7 Some experts are ____
about the future.

A fortune
B pessimist
C optimist
D pessimistic

8 Just imagine! Planes and trains
could be made ____ !

A crash
B to crash
C rise
D raise

9 Using the Internet, you can
find out about holiday ____ .

A offer
B offering
C offers
D offered

10 It is really possible to get all ____
of information from the Internet.

A kindly
B sorts
C sort
D type

11 In the years ____ we are going to see
an explosion of shopping on the Net.

A market
B to come
C come
D markets

12 It is ____ that in the future such
explosion is going to occur.

A clearly
B clear
C clean
D cleaned

13 Television will probably
____ in the future.

A appear
B approach
C disappoint
D disappear

14 The ____ service disappears with
the increasing use of e-mail.

A post
B postal
C posting
D posts

15 One of the things that worry
them is the activities of ___ .
A criminal
B cybercriminals
C cybercriminal
D a computer

16 ___ are really worried about
what the future brings.
A Leading
B Experts
C Engineering
D Technology

17 Even now, young ___ can get
into the computers of banks.
A monopoly
B hackers
C business
D managing

18 They are also able ___ the
computer systems of governments.
A to attack
B attacking
C attack
D attacked

19 Can you explain what else
they are ___ ?
A capable
B able to
C capacity
D capable of

20 In the future, this new form of
terrorism can really cause ___ .
A industrial
B chaos
C care
D certain

21 Such criminals may also
make planes and trains ___ .
A to crash
B crashing
C crash
D crashed

22 This has been a result
of the technological ___ .
A breaks
B breakthroughs
C super
D superior

23 Scientists expect to reach the level
of computer-generated ___ .
A reason
B reasoning
C reasonable
D resign

24 In the future, we will also
get ___ from the Net.
A entertain
B enters
C entering
D entertainment

25 We can all see that the use
of e-mail is constantly ___ .
A increasing
B breakthrough
C thoroughly
D break

26 Some ___ see our
future in virtual reality.
A special
B especially
C specialists
D specialist

27 It is the use of computers with
special sounds and ___ .
A imagine
B intellectual
C informs
D images

28 Virtual reality will inevitably
become part of ___ life.
A doing
B modern
C modernly
D fashions

29 This technology will also bring
studying in ___ schools.
A virtually
B virtual
C virtues
D virtue

30 Have you ___ !? The title of this
text is *The Future of Cyberspace*.
A forget
B forgive
C forgets
D forgotten

Test 7
THE LAWS OF MOTION AND UNIVERSAL GRAVITATION

1   Sir Isaac Newton is one of the
    most ___ scientists of all time.

    A prepare
    B profound
    C found
    D founder

2   He ___ and correlated many
    observations in mechanics.

    A impersonal
    B interprets
    C introduces
    D interpreted

3   Newton combined his
    results into three ___ laws.

    A fundamental
    B founded
    C funded
    D functionality

4   These three laws are referred to
    as Newton's laws of ___ .

    A motion
    B motivation
    C formulation
    D motive

5   His first law says that a body
    at rest remains ___ ...

    A rest
    B rests
    C at rest
    D to rest

6   ... while a body in motion
    continues to move at ___ speed.

    A connect
    B statement
    C correct
    D constant

7   Yes, that motion is
    continued along a ___ line.

    A straight
    B stated
    C freight
    D strict

8   Uniform motion is natural, and ___
    without the action of a resultant force.

    A maintains itself
    B maintains
    C motivates
    D moves itself

9   When a body is at rest, its ___
    is zero, it's easy to understand.

    A accelerated
    B acceptance
    C application
    D acceleration

10 The same ___ when it is moving at
    constant speed along a straight line.

    A truth
    B true
    C holds true
    D translates

11 A body accelerates only while
    some resultant force acts ___ it.

    A from
    B upon
    C up
    D down

12 The acceleration is inversely
    ___ to the mass of the body.

    A proper
    B proportional
    C property
    D prepared

13 The greater the resultant
    force – ___ the acceleration.

    A greater
    B bigger
    C faster
    D the greater

14 The acceleration of a body ___ in
    the direction of the resultant force.

    A takes part
    B takes place
    C takes a part
    D plays

15 All this – unless there is a ___
force acting upon the body.

A result
B real
C resultant
D consultant

16 The first part of this law is
___ from everyday experience.

A evident
B evidence
C eventual
D effort

17 For instance – a book ___
on a table remains at rest.

A position
B placed
C places
D stood

18 The second part of the law
is more difficult to ___ .

A visualize
B vivid
C virtual
D wonderful

19 A body ___ into motion and left
to itself – keeps on moving.

A put
B placed
C received
D set

20 Yes, it keeps on moving without
the action of any ___ force.

A farther
B forgiven
C forbidden
D further

21 There would be no reduction of
___ if no force acted upon the body.

A velocity
B vehicle
C tradition
D vulnerable

22 However, a retarding force is
always present in the nature of ___ .

A fry
B friction
C invention
D intervention

23 The ___ the mass –
the greater the acceleration.

A small
B little
C smallest
D smaller

24 The acceleration is ___
proportional to the resultant force.

A proposition
B proposal
C direction
D directly

25 Every action has its equal opposite
___ along the same straight line.

A complex
B reactor
C reaction
D complexity

26 Here *action* means the force that
one body ___ on a second body.

A exerts
B expects
C specialize
D speculates

27 Although equal and opposite, action
and reaction can ___ each other.

A balance
B restrict
C not lost
D never balance

28 The third law deals with the
___ forces between two bodies.

A moment
B mutually
C momentum
D mutual

29 He showed that every particle in
the ___ attracts every other particle.

A universe
B universal
C uniform
D unusual

30 Do you really understand
his Law of universal ___ ?

A specification
B dynamics
C gravitation
D distribution

Test 8

MARS, THE RED PLANET

1   Mars is called the Red Planet
    because it ___ looks red.
    A   actual
    B   activity
    C   alike
    D   actually

2   Mars, of course, is not only
    an ___ beautiful planet.
    A   extreme
    B   effective
    C   extremely
    D   excited

3   The question that fascinates us
    is: *Is there* ___ *Mars*?
    A   live
    B   life on
    C   life onto
    D   living

4   Venus is nearer, but it has
    a very hostile ___ .
    A   environment
    B   envy
    C   entertainment
    D   episode

5   That planet is covered
    in clouds of ___ gas.
    A   pose
    B   posing
    C   possess
    D   poison

6   The atmosphere of Mars
    is made up of ___ .
    A   carbon
    B   carbom dioxide
    C   oxide
    D   carbons

7   Mars has two ___ ,
    Phobos and Deimos.
    A   moons
    B   stars
    C   orbits
    D   meteors

8   It was then that 'Martians' ___
    science fiction for the first time.
    A   enter
    B   left
    C   lived
    D   entered

9   H. G. Wells' famous book *The War of
    the* ___ was published in 1898.
    A   World
    B   Worlds
    C   *Word*
    D   Worry

10 In that book, Martians are developed
    creatures that try to ___ planet Earth.
    A   take
    B   take away
    C   take over
    D   make up

11 The first ___ to get near Mars
    was *Mariner 4*.
    A   probe
    B   prove
    C   prospect
    D   protect

12 *Mariner 4* ___ past that planet
    in 1964 and took photos of it.
    A   flight
    B   fly
    C   flowed
    D   flew

13 After that, there were several
    ___ , with probes crashing.
    A   failures
    B   fail
    C   fall
    D   fill

14 The big ___ came with *Pathfinder*,
    which landed successfully.
    A   brake
    B   breaking
    C   thorough
    D   breakthrough

15 The surface is covered
    with ___ and huge volcanoes.
    A crate
    B crates
    C craters
    D grids

16 Towards the end of the 19th
    century ___ were improved.
    A videos
    B camcorders
    C satellites
    D telescopes

17 ___ could start then to observe
    the surface of that planet.
    A Airplanes
    B Astronomers
    C Adversaries
    D Aeronautic

18 The Italian astronomer Schiaparelli
    saw ___ on the surface.
    A a canal
    B canals
    C channel
    D channels

19 Schiaparelli's observations
    caused enormous ___ , of course.
    A interested
    B interest
    C interesting
    D interested in

20 Unfortunately, his work was
    ___ into English.
    A mistranslated
    B translations
    C mistaken
    D missed

21 Many other scientists ___
    the surface of that planet, too.
    A watched
    B looks
    C looking
    D observed

22 This triggered ___ about the
    possibility of life on Mars.
    A speculation
    B specification
    C specialization
    D selection

23 *Pathfinder* sent back ___
    photos of the surface of Mars.
    A spectacles
    B spectacle
    C spectacular
    D specify

24 The photos and the vehicle which
    ___ the area sparked great interest.
    A expedition
    B exploration
    C explored
    D exploded

25 The next probe ___ in 2001, with
    the task to provide communications.
    A was launched
    B launching
    C length
    D laundry

26 A meteorite found in Antarctica
    again ___ great interest in Mars.
    A caused
    B casual
    C causal
    D casing

27 A study in 2001 ___ the meteorite
    did contain chains of special crystals.
    A confirm
    B firmly
    C conference
    D confirmed

28 Do you think that there will be
    ___ missions to Mars soon?
    A screw
    B crewed
    C crew
    D crews

29 A manned ___ to Mars is right at the
    edge of our technological capacities.
    A missile
    B mission
    C missed
    D misuse

30 To ___ – in many ways Mars
    is our new frontier.
    A back up
    B sum
    C sum up
    D get up

Test 9
MOST COMMON PROBLEMS WITH R/C VEHICLES

1   What are the most ___ problems
    with R/C toy vehicles?
    A coming
    B commission
    C common
    D companion

2   What does the shortened
    form *R/C* ___ ?
    A make
    B stand
    C make up
    D stand for

3   For the very start, you should
    make ___ all batteries are fresh!
    A certain
    B certify
    C certainly
    D certificate

4   This toy is designed to accommodate
    Ni-Cd ___ batteries.
    A charge
    B change
    C changeable
    D rechargeable

5   In other cases you are advised
    to use high quality ___ batteries.
    A alkaline
    B all
    C alkali
    D alkalize

6   Incorrect battery ___ is
    a frequent cause of problem.
    A instalment
    B install
    C installation
    D instance

7   Be careful not to install
    them in ___ position!
    A reform
    B reverse
    C revise
    D adverse

8   Interference ___ can cause erratic
    behaviour or loss of control.
    A sources
    B source
    C scene
    D resources

9   Interference can sometimes
    come from ___ transmitters.
    A microwave
    B micron
    C macro
    D wave

10 High ___ transformers can
    also cause interference.
    A tall
    B vault
    C voltage
    D top

11 Yes, ___ telephones also
    have to be mentioned here.
    A cover
    B cords
    C seamless
    D cordless

12 If you ___ this type of problem,
    move to a better location.
    A exactly
    B effect
    C encounter
    D counter

13 Avoid other vehicles driving
    on ___ same as yours.
    A frequent
    B frequency
    C frequently
    D frequented

14 Wait until their transmitter is
    ___ before you start to drive.
    A turn off
    B turned off
    C turned down
    D turned around

15 Make certain the vehicle is
    turned off when ___ .
    A in use
    B using
    C used
    D not in use

16 To prevent battery failure, also
    be sure to turn off the ___ .
    A transmission
    B emission
    C emit
    D transmitter

17 The vehicle can't be driven
    beyond radio signal ___ .
    A charge
    B range
    C rank
    D strange

18 This inevitably leads
    to ___ of control.
    A lost
    B losing
    C loss
    D loose

19 Some toy cars are specifically
    ___ for long range racing.
    A determine
    B design
    C designed
    D destroyed

20 Alkaline batteries generally do not
    ___ longer than 25 to 40 minutes.
    A lost
    B last
    C lasting
    D lets

21 In other words, their ___
    time is about half an hour.
    A running
    B run
    C served
    D useful

22 This all means that
    batteries must ___ often.
    A replace
    B replacement
    C displaced
    D be replaced

23 Drive on dry surfaces,
    avoid ___ areas.
    A dump
    B damp
    C dumb
    D down

24 Be careful and try to ___
    your vehicle delicately.
    A help
    B handle
    C enable
    D handed

25 You should by all means
    avoid driving into ___ .
    A obstacle
    B obstacled
    C obstacles
    D frequencies

26 Remember: dry, smooth, flat
    and ___ surfaces are the safest.
    A clean
    B clear
    C cleaning
    D cleared

27 Rough surfaces are only for toys
    ___ designed for "off-road" use.
    A specify
    B specified
    C sometimes
    D specifically

28 Do you agree that there are
    people who ___ their toy vehicles?
    A difficult to use
    B negligent
    C easy to use
    D abuse

29 Do not ___ the car to the
    store where purchased!
    A overturn
    B turn over
    C brought
    D return

30 For problems of service, please
    contact our ___ Center.
    A Prepare
    B Repair
    C Proposed
    D Preparations

Test 10
THE ANALYTICAL MIND – A PERFECT COMPUTER

1 The human mind can be considered
to have three major ___ .
A divide
B divisions
C divides
D determines

2 The first of the three can
be called the ___ *mind*.
A analysis
B analyse
C analyses
D analytical

3 Consider the analytical mind
as a ___ machine!
A computer
B computer's
C computers
D computing

4 This ___ is easy to make.
It is very logical.
A analogy
B analysing
C abuse
D anatomy

5 The analytical mind is more
fantastically capable than any ___ .
A computation
B computer's
C computers
D computing machine

6 In addition – it is ___
more elaborate.
A infinitives
B infinitely
C fine
D infinitive

7 The analytical mind can also
be called the ___ *mind*.
A computational
B computations
C computing
D computer system

8 What would you want in
a ___ of that kind?
A machines
B machinery
C appliance
D machine

9 It really resembles
the best computer ___ !
A awaiting
B available
C able
D admirable

10 The action of this human mind
segment is that of an ___ .
A analyzer
B analyzed
C fusion
D experimental

11 It can and does do
all the ___ of a computer.
A trick
B threat
C tricky
D tricks

12 And over and above that – it
directs the ___ of computers.
A buildings
B builder
C constructions
D building

13 It is also as ___ right
as any computer ever was.
A through
B thought
C thoroughly
D tough

14 It is not just a *good* computer,
it is a ___ computer!
A perfect
B perfection
C prefer
D partly

15 This mind may live
in the ___ lobes.
A prefrontal
B preliminary
C prestigeous
D present

16 This means – in the ___ of the
brain directly behind the forehead.
A portion
B portion's
C portrait
D partition

17 We do not know this for certain.
There is some ___ of that.
A kick
B hoping
C hint
D stick

18 However, this is a problem
of ___ , we can agree to that.
A strong
B structure
C structural
D static

19 We can conclude that the
analytical mind ___ data.
A analyze
B analyzes
C analyses
D analysis

20 The analytical mind shows
evidence of being ___ .
A organism
B organisation
C organ
D an organ

21 The full ___ knowledge of it must
come after we know what it does.
A structural
B structure
C architecture
D architect

22 It ___ as you would expect any
good computing machine to behave.
A behaves
B behaviour
C bee hive
D behaving

23 It is a computer that
never ___ a mistake!
A radiate
B make
C forgive
D makes

24 It cannot ___ in any way so long as
a human being is reasonably intact.
A or
B err
C are
D error

25 Unless something has carried away
___ of his mental equipment!
A peace
B piece
C price
D a piece

26 It ___ everything on the basis
that it cannot make an error.
A work
B worked up
C working
D works out

27 Imagine! That person has
never been taught ___ .
A an addition
B added
C ads
D to add

28 A computer is just as good
as the data on which it ___ .
A operate
B operation
C operate on
D operates

29 In addition to *analytical* mind, we can
speak of a ___ mind, too.
A reaction
B reactor
C reactive
D recreation

30 Of course, there is also
the division called the ___ mind.
A somatic
B sounding
C sympathetic
D sophistication

108

Test 11
HOW STATISTICS CAN FOOL YOU

1   Is it true that
    ___ can fool us?
    A static
    B statics
    C statistically
    D statistics

2   Mark Twain once said that
    there were three kinds of ___ .
    A lay
    B lied
    C laid
    D lies

3   Very often, its sources
    are learned ___ .
    A public
    B publicity
    C publications
    D audience

4   They ___ considerably
    in many respects.
    A different
    B differ
    C to differ
    D offer different

5   However, they have
    many things ___ .
    A common
    B in common
    C commons
    D commonly

6   Neither of them is likely
    ___ of flat lies!
    A compose
    B to be composed
    C to compose
    D composers

7   ___ may be the value of some
    information, often it is not a lie.
    A Which
    B What
    C Where
    D Whatever

8   A hundred per cent ___
    very large indeed.
    A sound
    B sounding
    C saved
    D sounds

9   Forget those figures! Statistically
    speaking, they are ___ .
    A significant
    B not significant
    C able
    D disable

10 Statistics is ___ the easiest
    branch of mathematics.
    A means
    B this means
    C meaning
    D by no means

11 The normal use of
    statistics is ___ trends.
    A indication
    B indicate
    C to be informed
    D to indicate

12 Statisticians find, or rather
    ___ , interesting things to study.
    A select
    B serve
    C save
    D hope

13 Such ___ occur at
    the same time.
    A phenomenon
    B phenomena
    C thoroughly
    D phenomenal

14 At the same time means
    more or less ___ .
    A simultaneously
    B simultaneous
    C stimulus
    D stimuli

15 Statistics can be ___
in a number of ways.
A leading
B mystery
C misleading
D mistake

16 They have to offer a
___ selection of cases.
A portion
B random
C rather
D partially

17 They also have ___ a very
large selection of cases.
A to cover
B covering
C is to cover
D to be covered

18 Wait! We should not hurry
___ conclusions immediately.
A draw
B drawing
C to draw
D drawers

19 Try to be careful with
very ___ conclusions!
A far
B far-reaching
C reaching
D far away

20 Let us suppose you now
learn some more ___ .
A organism
B details
C detailed
D difference

21 During the year under ___
important things happened.
A review
B reviewed
C view
D reconstruction

22 That information will surely
give you ___ .
A pace
B piece
C place
D pause

23 Very often, things and events
are to be ___ statistically.
A dealing
B dealt
C dealt with
D dealing in

24 It is important to establish some
___ connection between things.
A causal
B caused
C cause
D causing

25 This, in fact, is the
___ requirement.
A express
B essence
C exclusivity
D essential

26 Without that, statistical
treatment is ___ of time.
A work
B wait
C waist
D waste

27 What more, it can also be
understood as ___ .
A distribute
B display
C dishonest
D disturb

28 Some things are only
___ of some other things.
A efficient
B effective
C effect
D effects

29 May it not be ___
coincidental?
A pure
B proof
C present
D purely

30 What if things are produced
by some ___ cause?
A suspecting
B unsuspected
C suspension
D suspense

Test 12
A LANDMARK SCIENCE FICTION FILM

1 Haven't you seen that
___ science fiction film yet?
A marking
B lands
C mark
D landmark

2 *2001: Space Odyssey*
originally ___ in 1968.
A brought
B tried
C get
D came out

3 A lot of people did not
like it at ___ time.
A then
B a
C an
D that

4 They did not like it because
they couldn't ___ .
A make it
B made it
C make it out
D make it up

5 Many people found
the film strange and ___ .
A common
B cooperate
C confusing
D confusingly

6 It is totally ___ most
science fiction films.
A liked
B as
C unlike
D liking

7 There is little action,
but the director ___ it.
A made up
B makes up
C makes up with
D made up for

8 The third part pf the film
is about a ___ to Jupiter.
A tip
B trip
C slip
D sweep

9 Five men are on a space
___ to that planet.
A missile
B missed
C mist
D mission

10 Three of them
are in ___ .
A hibernate
B hibernated
C hibernating
D hibernation

11 While they are hibernating,
the other two are ___ the ship.
A looking after
B looked into
C loooking away
D looked out

12 It would be ___ to say that the
new supercomputer is in charge.
A better
B the best
C well
D kindly

13 However, after a while, the
computer begins to act ___ .
A strange
B phenomena
C stranger
D strangely

14 At one moment HAL detected a
serious problem in the ___ .
A spaceship
B ship's
C spacing
D spaced

15 Another famous piece
of music is played ___ slowly.

A defect
B master
C liberal
D deliberately

16 It is not easy to explain
what the film ___ .

A deals
B dealing
C is about
D is afraid

17 It could be said that it is
___ with an alien civilisation.

A to make
B to do
C doing
D standing

18 The truth is that you never
___ see any aliens in the film.

A actual
B actually
C exact
D right

19 A group of ape-men
found an enormous ___ .

A monotony
B monolith
C method
D monsters

20 That machine has been sent
to us by an ___ alien civilisation.

A organisation
B advanced
C advancement
D organizing

21 A scientist now goes to the Moon
to ___ two black monoliths.

A revive
B refinery
C investigate
D restart

22 The block is really a ___ kind of
machine that has been sent to Earth.

A strong
B straight
C stranger
D strange

23 It says that the ship's ___
syste ms are going to fall.

A communicate
B communicates
C communication
D communicated

24 Then, the 9000 computer ___
Earth says there's nothing wrong.

A back
B on
C back on
D back up

25 It becomes ___ that HAL
has made a mistake.

A obvious
B obviously
C obliged
D optimist

26 At that moment Dave and Frank
began to get worried ___ HAL.

A for
B for the
C with the
D about

27 They have started thinking
about ___ the supercomputer.

A distributing
B disconnecting
C deciding
D discovering

28 What they do not know is
that HAL can hear them ___ .

A talked
B speak
C spoke
D talking

29 HAL is the only one on the
ship who knows the ___ .

A pure mission
B real mission
C missiles
D purify

30 The next part of the film
happens ___ of years later.

A million and million
B millions and millions
C million and millions
D million and billions

Test 13

WHAT MACHINES CAN, AND CAN NOT, DO

1   This text is about what
    ___ can, and can not, do.
    A machines
    B mechanical
    C making
    D mechanic

2   It is the Age of Machinery,
    in every ___ of that word.
    A stay
    B sense
    C sensual
    D space

3   Who talks about a *Thinking
    Machine* – doesn't know what ___ is.
    A thinks
    B think
    C thinking
    D thoughts

4   A machine is a ___
    operated by a man.
    A took
    B stool
    C tool
    D tools

5   If it is in ___ working order,
    it carries out its instructions.
    A sane
    B dangerous
    C sound
    D sounding

6   It carries out its instructions
    as efficiently as its ___ directs it.
    A director
    B operator
    C monitor
    D screen

7   Very often we ___ that
    machines don't 'make mistakes'.
    A are told
    B has told
    C was telling
    D made up for

8   There has been a lot of ___
    about machinery.
    A mistaking
    B misunderstanding
    C misleading
    D missing

9   A lot of it ___ from
    the misuse of metaphors.
    A rise
    B rising
    C raise
    D arises

10 We often hear that
    machines have ___ .
    A memories
    B memoirs
    C materials
    D methods

11 We can also hear that
    machines can make ___ .
    A decisive
    B defect
    C deviation
    D decisions

12 What we mean in fact is
    that they can ___ information.
    A store
    B start
    C starter
    D storey

13 The point is that machines
    ___ to stimuli.
    A correspond
    B respond
    C responsible
    D responsibility

14 The thermostat is a useful and
    valuable ___ .
    A inventor
    B invitation
    C investing
    D invention

15 A not ___ hypothesis is that
there are some errors in this text.
A potential
B continual
C impersonal
D impossible

16 Yes, of course, some errors
may have ___ into this text.
A creep
B creeping
C crew
D crept

17 What are you going to do? Tell
the readers that___ has failed?
A to keyboard
B keyboarder
C the keyboard
D key board

18 Remember: It is not keyboards
that make ___ mistakes!
A spell
B spin
C spinning
D spelling

19 People who ___ texts
sometimes make mistakes.
A type
B typing
C typewriter
D typist

20 Electronic machinery has made
fantastic ___ in the recent years.
A printing
B prospect
C advancement
D progress

21 There will never be a
breakthrough into ___ activity.
A conscience
B conscious
C conscientious
D consciousness

22 When you get down to ___ , a
computer is an improved abacus!
A funds
B funding
C fundamentalist
D fundamentals

23 Of course, it does not *decide*
___ the heat when necessary.
A to switch
B a switch
C switching
D to switch off

24 Electronic machinery
works at ___ speed.
A lights
B lighter
C lightning
D lighting

25 Such machinery can reply to
questions in ___ seconds.
A matter
B matter of
C matters
D a matter of

26 The heat is switched off when
a certain temperature ___ .
A is reached
B reaching
C is reaching
D is touched

27 Such questions might ___
a team of experts for years.
A emphasise
B employed
C employee
D engage

28 When we say *experts*,
here we mean ___ .
A mathematics
B mechanics
C mathematicians
D physics

29 The machine, of course,
has to be ___ .
A programming
B programmed
C a program
D a programme

30 The question is first ___
in mathematical language.
A frames
B framing
C froze
D framed

Test 14
AN ABSOLUTELY AMAZING ORGAN

1 We all agree that it is
   an ___ amazing organ!
   A absolute
   B absorbing
   C absent
   D absolutely

2 The brain, we know that,
   ___ of grey and white matter.
   A consists
   B connects
   C continues
   D compares

3 It ___ just over a kilo
   – just imagine that!
   A weights
   B weighs
   C weight
   D weighing

4 However, this is
   a very ___ kilo!
   A specially
   B especially
   C specialty
   D special

5 The brain uses twenty
   percent of the body's ___ .
   A energetics
   B energetically
   C energy
   D energetic

6 And, yes, it ___ over
   one hundred billion cells.
   A connects
   B container
   C completes
   D contains

7 Neurons, or ___ , are connected
   by electrical impulses.
   A nerve cells
   B nervousness
   C nervous
   D nerve

8 Different areas of the brain are
   responsible for different ___ .
   A mistaking
   B functions
   C fractions
   D fiction

9 Neuroscientists have ___
   different areas of the brain.
   A made
   B trapped
   C mapped
   D stepped

10 We now know which parts
    of the brain are ___ to what.
    A relates
    B relate
    C related
    D relatively

11 A good example of this can be
    seen in people who have lost ___ .
    A limb
    B left
    C a limb
    D lift

12 Specific areas of our brain
    ___ all our movements.
    A counting
    B control
    C computer
    D count

13 To ___ an arm, electronic
    impulses are needed.
    A put
    B give out
    C put up
    D put away

14 It is really quite a
    complicated ___ .
    A operate
    B operated on
    C operator
    D operation

15 The brain sends messages
using electrical ___ .
A impulse
B pulse
C toner
D impulses

16 This means that it works
the same way a computer___ .
A work
B worker
C working
D works

17 Possible connections in
one brain are ___ .
A less than a number
B numberless
C numbered
D numerical

18 Remember: There are more of
them then there are atoms ___ !
A universal
B in the universe
C in a universe
D university

19 This really makes a normal
computer look very ___ .
A simplify
B simple
C simplicity
D simplification

20 Neuroscientists study the
brain and the nervous ___ .
A systems
B systemic
C systematically
D system

21 They have ___ a lot
about it in recent decades.
A learned
B learning
C learnt
D learners

22 They are like explorers
___ the world.
A explicit
B express
C exposing
D exploring

23 Some areas of the brain could
be compared to ___ film studios.
A minimum
B miniature
C minimally
D minimize

24 They make a film and soundtrack
of what is happening ___ us.
A around
B afraid
C away
D await

25 It is not our ears that ___ ,
but our brains.
A concentration
B listen
C hearing
D attention

26 It is not our eyes that ___ ,
but our brains.
A looking
B watching
C see
D sawing

27 Our eyes and ears send
___ all the time.
A symbols
B signals
C simple
D symptoms

28 It is our brain that
___ the picture of the outside world.
A construction
B builds up
C creative
D building

29 The brain ___
all these signals.
A programming
B interpretation
C internal
D interprets

30 There is an area for our first
language, and an area for a ___ one.
A foreigner
B foreign
C friend
D foreigner's

Test 15

A BIT TOO HOT, I'M AFRAID!

1   It is a bit too ___ ,
    I'm afraid!
    A hate
    B heat
    C hot
    D hut

2   Reports being ___ all the time
    confirm global climate change.
    A publicly
    B audience
    C publishing
    D published

3   For the last three decades
    temperatures have been ___ .
    A above
    B averaged
    C above average
    D averaging

4   The global temperature
    has risen ___ since 1910.
    A specially
    B steadily
    C stealthily
    D seemingly

5   This is ___ the increased
    burning of fossil fuels.
    A owl
    B owned
    C owed
    D owing to

6   This means that ___ of
    carbon dioxide have increased.
    A programmes
    B emissions
    C emit
    D programs

7   The increase in the ___ century
    was only 0.6 deg. centigrade.
    A twenty
    B twentieth
    C two
    D twelve

8   This has actually meant
    ___ changes in climate.
    A mayor
    B major
    C majority
    D main

9   Both the Arctic and Antarctic
    ___ are melting.
    A ice caps
    B ice
    C icing
    D iced

10 Computer forecasts ___ that
    global warming could speed up.
    A predict
    B prepare
    C relate
    D propose

11 The ___ forecasts speak
    about new problems.
    A last
    B late
    C latter
    D latest

12 The population of giant pandas
    is around 1,000 owing to ___ .
    A forestry
    B deforestation
    C deformation
    D dedication

13 The good news is that now there
    are 11,000 white rhinos ___ .
    A wild
    B the wild
    C wilderness
    D in the wild

14 ___ suggest that the world's
    growth is beginning to slow down.
    A Figured
    B Figurines
    C Figurative
    D Figures

15 This will have unforeseen
___ for the future.
A conclusion
B conferences
C consequences
D competences

16 Recently ___ statistics also show
the number of endangered species.
A released
B relieved
C relying
D reflexion

17 The 'red list' tells us about the
species on the brink of ___ .
A extinction
B explanation
C evacuation
D extinct

18 This list has ___ dramatically
in the last few years.
A grew
B growing
C grown
D grown up

19 Over ___ of the world's
reptiles are threatened.
A quarter
B quarterly
C a quarter
D quarry

20 Also threatened are ___
of the world's amphibians.
A a fifth
B fifth
C sixtieth
D sixteenth

21 All these animals are threatened
by the ___ of their habitats.
A construction
B destruction
C destroy
D constructive

22 The ___ of tigers
is down to 5,000.
A populated
B popular
C popularity
D population

23 World population has
___ since the year 1960.
A double
B doubled
C doubling
D troubling

24 The growth has mainly been
in the ___ world.
A divide
B develop
C distribution
D developing

25 In many African countries 40%
of the population is under ___ .
A fifteen
B fifteenth
C fifth
D fiftieth

26 The world population will
have ___ around 2070.
A stable
B stability
C stabilised
D stubborn

27 Unfortunately, the number of
poor people in the world is ___ .
A creased
B increase
C inside
D increasing

28 Poor people ___ one third
of the world's population!
A making
B makes
C make
D make up

29 The world has grown richer,
but the number of the poor ___ !
A going up
B going down
C is going up
D going wrong

30 This situation is really
___ , isn't it?
A worry
B worrying
C worried
D worries

LANDMARKS OF SCIENCE IN THE 20th CENTURY

1   In the summer of 1905, he was
    sitting at home after ___ work.
    A day's
    B day
    C date
    D a day's

2   While rocking his baby,
    he thought something ___ .
    A publicly
    B under
    C over
    D always

3   And... yes!
    It ___ him suddenly!
    A came
    B came to
    C come to
    D coming to

4   The famous ___
    $e = mc^2$ was born.
    A equal
    B equality
    C equate
    D equation

5   That expression would later
    change our ___ of the universe.
    A understatement
    B understanding
    C understand
    D standing under

6   However, it also helped
    to create a ___ bomb.
    A nuclear
    B nucleus
    C kernel
    D nuclei

7   He was aware of Marie Curie's
    research ___ radioactivity.
    A at
    B about
    C off
    D into

8   Edwin Hubble used the most
    ___ telescope of that time.
    A high power
    B highly
    C high-powered
    D poor

9   His observation of nebulae
    was ___ slow.
    A pains
    B painstaking
    C taken
    D painstakingly

10 Nebulae are small patches of
    light that ___ outside our galaxy.
    A apply
    B apprentice
    C appease
    D appear

11 Having returned from the War,
    he started work at an ___ .
    A observation
    B observed
    C observatory
    D observing

12 He was on the brink of making
    a great ___ breakthrough.
    A astronomy
    B asterisk
    C astronomical
    D astronomers

13 In fact that was the ___
    breakthrough of the century.
    A great
    B greatest
    C vast
    D wide

14 It was the famous Mount Wilson
    Observatory ___ California.
    A in
    B at
    C from
    D into

15 However, he had been
working ___ his own.
A at
B on
C for
D after

16 A small ___ of mass can produce
an enormous amount of energy.
A peace
B pieces
C place
D piece

17 Yes, an ___ amount
of energy can be produced.
A believed
B unbelievable
C belief
D beliefs

18 Not even time, mass
or length are ___ .
A connect
B constantly
C constable
D constant

19 Einstein demonstrated that
in his theory of ___ .
A relatives
B relative
C relativity
D relatively

20 Time, mass or length vary
according to our ___ of them.
A prospect
B prescribe
C prescription
D perspective

21 People moving at the speed of light
would ___ much heavier.
A appear
B apparatus
C appearance
D apply

22 They would seem
to move in ___ .
A slowed motion
B motive
C slowly
D slow motion

23 He discovered that these nebulae
were ___ galaxies like our own.
A fact
B factors
C in the fact
D in fact

24 hey are millions of
___ years away from us.
A lightly
B lighted
C lighting
D light

25 The universe was vastly larger
than had previuosly been ___ .
A teach
B tech
C thought
D thoughts

26 Then, Hubble proved that
the universe is actually ___ .
A expensive
B expanding
C explaining
D expressing

27 The farther away the galaxies
are, the faster they ___ .
A moved
B motion
C motionless
D move

28 A machine was needed to do
some incredibly complex ___ .
A calculations
B calculator
C calculate
D counter

29 ENIAC was the world's first
computer. It was ___ !
A hum
B hug
C huge
D hop

30 The ENIAC project failed
to meet its original ___ .
A object
B subject
C predicate
D objective

Test 17
TO REMEMBER ABOUT MATHEMATICS...

1   There are many important
    things ___ about mathematics.
    A remembering
    B to remember
    C forget
    D remind

2   Mathematics is not simply
    a matter of ___ numerals.
    A writing down
    B wrote
    C writing off
    D to write

3   Mathematics is more
    a way of ___ .
    A taught
    B thought
    C thinks
    D thinking

4   Playing a game of cards is,
    of course, ___ mathematics.
    A use
    B using
    C usefully
    D used

5   You know ___ mathematics,
    I agree.
    A element
    B elemental
    C elementary
    D elements

6   Have you ___ yourself with
    the Greek alphabet yet?
    A family
    B familiarized
    C familiar
    D family's

7   You use difficult mathematical
    ___ every day.
    A process
    B procedures
    C procedure
    D processed

8   Some of the conditions ___ by the
    time you lodge your information.
    A change
    B having changed
    C choose
    D cheer

9   A rifle-shooting competitor
    estimates and ___ wind.
    A waits
    B allows for
    C applies
    D allowances

10 The drop in the parabolic ___
    is the result of gravity.
    A curve
    B curved
    C curvilinear
    D carve

11 Of course, he does not
    call himself ___ .
    A mathematics
    B mathematical
    C mathematician's
    D a mathematician

12 Thank God you have
    ___ that perilous ordeal.
    A surface
    B surfing
    C survival
    D survived

13 You may not ___ of the amount
    of calculations you do every day.
    A be free
    B conscious
    C awareness
    D be aware

14 You have estimated
    the speed of the cars ___ .
    A appear
    B approaching
    C applying
    D reproaching

15 You use such procedures
every day without ___ .
A realize
B realized that
C realistically
D realizing it

16 Knowledge of ___ is required
for a game of billiards.
A geometrical
B geometry
C geothermal
D geodesic

17 Think of that knowledge, though it be
___ knowledge.
A unconscious
B consciousness
C conscience
D disconnected

18 Complicated ___ are needed
to hit an archery target.
A calculate
B calculated
C calculation
D calculations

19 Complicated ___ are
also needed, of course.
A estimated
B estimate
C estimates
D stimulates

20 You must ___ the size
and distance of the target.
A suffer
B judge
C compete
D complain

21 Also think about the weight of the
arrow as against the estimated ___ !
A velocity
B fast
C quick
D rapidly

22 Even if you ___ all this data into a
computer, you are disappointed.
A fed
B feed
C fight
D fly

23 Be careful! There are cars
speeding from both ___ .
A directly
B diversity
C direction
D directions

24 Apart from using the estimates
___ , you also use trigonometry.
A corrections
B correct
C corrected
D correctly

25 You ___ this feat daily
with repeated success!
A acceptance
B complicated
C accomplish
D acclamation

26 How do you ___ this result?
Do tell us, please!
A application
B achievement
C across
D achieve

27 Each one of us has
a computer ___ his skull.
A built in
B building
C constructed
D builders

28 That built-in computer is
a very ___ instrument indeed.
A relying
B lying
C laying
D reliable

29 It will never ___ unless you
feed it the wrong information.
A mistakes
B mistaken
C make a mistake
D mistakenly

30 Do you ___ that there are many
interesting things about maths?
A appear
B agree
C apply
D admire

Test 18
DEADLY NUCLEAR WASTE UNDER REC CENTER?

1   Deadly nuclear ___ was found
    under a recreation center!?

    A waste
    B wasted
    C waist
    D waistcoat

2   In the ___ 1970s,
    Mr. Hirsch was a professor.

    A later
    B late
    C latest
    D last

3   Yes, at that time Mr. Dan Hirsch
    was ___ university professor.

    A a
    B an
    C any
    D if

4   He heard from some of his
    students a ___ story.

    A horrify
    B horrifying
    C horrified
    D scarcely

5   The story said that a rec center
    was sitting ___ a dark secret!

    A atop
    B a top
    C top
    D topped

6   That center was in Brentwood,
    a ___ of Los Angeles.

    A suburb
    B suburban
    C subsequent
    D subscribe

7   There was talk about quiet ___
    of nuclear waste into a landfill.

    A dump
    B procedures
    C dumping
    D filling

8   The problem is that this stuff
    sticks ___ for hundreds of years.

    A around
    B another
    C rounded
    D round

9   A bizzare ___ with a Brentwood
    lobby group followed.

    A confrontation
    B front
    C confronted
    D comprehensive

10 Baseball fields were to be built
    on the radioactive real ___ .

    A state
    B stations
    C estate
    D stationery

11 These people, ___ parents of local
    kids, didn't believe the stories.

    A wealthy
    B well
    C wealth
    D where

12 Was it some ___ move
    to scare away the competition?

    A developing
    B developer's
    C develops
    D underdeveloped

13 The abbreviation NRC ___ the
    Nuclear Regulatory Commission.

    A stands free
    B stays there
    C stuffed
    D stands for

14 At one point the NRC
    was called in ___ .

    A to investigate
    B to interpret
    C for investigation
    D for the purpose of

15 The ___ of the hospital
    were responsible.
    A stuff
    B staff
    C stuffed
    D starch

16 Hirsch formed a coalition of his
    students to look into the ___ .
    A charged
    B charges
    C charging
    D changed

17 They soon ___ , of course,
    that the rumours were true.
    A found
    B foundations
    C founded
    D finding

18 The hospital had indeed used
    the area as ___ for waste.
    A damp
    B a dump
    C dumping
    D pumping

19 They ___ a paper trail
    indicating these facts.
    A covered
    B uncovered
    C covering
    D coverage

20 he waste dumped was from
    the ___ therapy program.
    A radiate
    B radiator
    C erase
    D radiation

21 The main concern
    here is about the ___ .
    A soil
    B salt
    C sold
    D sale

22 The concern was, in fact,
    about the ___ .
    A vegetation
    B vegatative
    C vegetate
    D veterinary

23 First they swept the area
    with the Geiger ___ .
    A counter
    B counting
    C compression
    D complication

24 After that first step,
    the NRC ___ the area safe!
    A promoted
    B protected
    C pronounced
    D proceeded

25 LAPD stands for: Los Angeles
    Police ___ .
    A Departure
    B Determination
    C Deportation
    D Department

26 A LAPD helicopter flew him over
    the property with an ___ camera.
    A ultrasound
    B infrared
    C ultraviolet
    D infrastructure

27 In the ___ someone had gone
    over the area with a bulldozer.
    A mean time
    B meaning the time
    C meaningless
    D meantime

28 All vegetation had been
    completely ___ !
    A looked out
    B throughout
    C wiped out
    D put out

29 They didn't take the simple and
    obvious step of ___ soil samples.
    A obtaining
    B reminding
    C remaining
    D complaining

30 If you are the ___ type, limit your
    visits to that Recreation Center!
    A caused
    B casuals
    C cautious
    D causeless

Test 19
SANTA CRUZ MYSTERY SPOT

1 The laws of physics
   do not seem ___ there.
   A application
   B applicative
   C having applied
   D to apply

2 Here water flows ___ .
   Just imagine that!
   A skyward
   B toward
   C towards
   D the ward

3 To let you see this place
   they charge ___ , of course!
   A address
   B admit
   C admission
   D admiration

4 They say people can
   ___ walk up walls there!
   A active
   B actually
   C afraid
   D acquire

5 Have you ever heard
   of such ___ activity?
   A anomalous
   B anomaly
   C another
   D afraid

6 And what do you do if you
   discover a ___ like this?
   A places
   B cite
   C site
   D sit

7 Yes, this is the ___
   Santa Cruz Mystery Spot.
   A calling
   B such called
   C calls
   D so-called

8 Do you know the___
   of *Santa Cruz* in Spanish?
   A means
   B meaning
   C meaningful
   D meaningless

9 Don't miss visiting Berkeley,
   fifty miles ___ from here!
   A in the north
   B the north
   C to the north
   D northern

10 The Mystery Spot is a ___
   of land just north of the city.
   A parcel
   B patch
   C place
   D pond

11 This is a section of land where
   the laws of physics are ___ .
   A suspense
   B suspension
   C tension
   D suspended

12 The laws of gravity and ___
   obviously do not apply there!
   A prospect
   B prospector
   C prosperity
   D perspective

13 This is one of North America's
   most famous and visited ___ .
   A vortices
   B vortex
   C vertical
   D variety

14 ___ , the land around the spot
   served as a summer-cabin site.
   A Original
   B Originally
   C Originate
   D Origins

15 Has somebody ___ this just
    to disorient the hapless tourist?
    A destruction
    B project
    C projectors
    D designed

16 Such places ___ all that
    science has taught us!
    A believe
    B belittle
    C belly
    D belie

17 Have you learned about
    the way the universe ___ ?
    A operations
    B operates
    C in operation
    D operative

18 You're right!
    We can not really say ___ ...
    A sure
    B assured
    C surely
    D for sure

19 Santa Cruz is a seaside
    ___ and college town.
    A reserve
    B to resort
    C restless
    D resort

20 The local culture of that town
    seems to be rather ___ .
    A ad
    B add
    C odd
    D oddly

21 There you can ___ a vast
    array of bohemian subcultures.
    A notion
    B notify
    C nonsense
    D note

22 We have visited both Santa Cruz
    and its ___ university city, Berkeley.
    A brother
    B father
    C sister
    D mother

23 When ___ came to this spot,
    they found a lot of strange things.
    A surprises
    B surveyors
    C surfaces
    D surveys

24 They attempted ___ the lot,
    but it proved to be difficult.
    A to chart
    B charts
    C card
    D map

25 Their instruments simply
    could not give accurate ___ .
    A ready
    B readiness
    C readers
    D readings

26 The story ___ that they found
    it impossible to work there!
    A talks
    B tells
    C goes
    D speaks

27 A strange ___ seemed to be
    trying to push them off-balance.
    A forceful
    B power
    C powerful
    D force

28 The owners then ___ their
    plan to develop the land.
    A application
    B abandoned
    C afterwards
    D affected

29 Instead, they ___ the site
    as a tourist attraction.
    A opened
    B opened up
    C invented
    D makes up

30 They still ___ that strange
    forces are at play on the hill.
    A clay
    B call
    C calling
    D claim

Test 20
THE MOONRAKER

1   It was like being inside the
    ___ barrel of a huge gun.
    A polished
    B polite
    C pole
    D polar

2   From the floor there
    rose ___ metal walls.
    A circle
    B circular
    C circus
    D searching

3   Near the top of these he
    and Drax ___ like two flies.
    A clings
    B clinging
    C clay
    D clung

4   The ___ itself was
    about thirty feet wide.
    A shift
    B sharp
    C shaft
    D shine

5   Through the ___ of it
    soared a metal pencil.
    A central
    B centre
    C centrally
    D circularly

6   That metal pencil was
    made of ___ chromium.
    A glow
    B glistening
    C glue
    D glisten

7   Its point seemed to graze the
    roof twenty feet ___ their heads.
    A after
    B always
    C ahead
    D above

8   Where these touched the rocket,
    small ___ doors stood open.
    A success
    B appear
    C access
    D activate

9   The small doors stood open
    in the steel ___ of the rocket.
    A skin
    B spin
    C spot
    D show

10 A man crawled out of one
    door on to the narrow ___ .
    A place
    B platform
    C play
    D swaying

11 He closed the door behind
    him with a ___ hand.
    A glowed
    B gloves
    C gloved
    D glorious

12 He walked along the narrow
    bridge to the wall and turned ___ .
    A handed
    B handle
    C handling
    D a handle

13 Suddenly, a sharp ___
    of machinery could be heard.
    A wine
    B where
    C whine
    D windy

14 After that the gantry took its
    padded hand ___ the rocket.
    A of
    B off
    C offer
    D often

15 The shimmering ___
    rested on a blunt cone.
    A project
    B prospect
    C perspective
    D projectile

16 That blunt cone was made
    of strangely shaped ___ .
    A stole
    B steal
    C stolen
    D steel

17 It rose from the floor between the
    tips of three back-swept delta ___ .
    A fines
    B fins
    C finds
    D fires

18 To him they looked as ___
    as unused surgeons' scalpels.
    A sharp
    B sure
    C shade
    D straw

19 He was ___ by the silken sheen
    of the fifty feet of polished steel.
    A impersonal
    B impressed
    C impression
    D impressive

20 The spidery fingers of two light
    gantries ___ from the walls.
    A stayed
    B stood
    C stood out
    D time out

21 These fingers ___ the waist
    of the rocket.
    A catch
    B cough
    C catcher
    D clasped

22 They held the waist of the rocket
    between thick pads of ___ .
    A rub
    B fine rubbing
    C foam-rubber
    D foaming

23 Soon the whine altered
    to a much ___ tone.
    A depth
    B deep
    C dip
    D deeper

24 Immediately after that the
    gantry slowly ___ in on itself.
    A mechanical
    B telescoped
    C telescope
    D merged

25 Then it reached out
    again and ___ the rocket.
    A size
    B sizzle
    C seizes
    D seized

26 This time it held the rocket
    some ten feet ___ down.
    A slow
    B slower
    C lower
    D lowly

27 Its ___ crawled out along its
    arm and opened another door.
    A operate
    B operator
    C operating
    D proper

28 A moment later that
    man ___ inside.
    A disappeared
    B disturbed
    C distorted
    D distant

29 He was probably ___ the
    fuel-feed from the after tanks.
    A cheque
    B checked
    C choosing
    D checking

30 It was easy to talk – there was
    hardly ___ in the great steel shaft.
    A a sound
    B sounding
    C sounds
    D a sonar

128

Test 21
ELECTROMAGNETIC WAVES

1 Electromagnetic waves come
from a number of different ___ .
A saves
B sources
C forces
D portions

2 They are the effect of ___
electric and magnetic fields.
A complicated
B oscillating
C oscillated
D cylindrical

3 You certainly know that
these have different ___ .
A wavelengths
B wave's length
C waves' length
D waving

4 They all travel through free space,
i. e. ___ , at an enormous speed.
A vacant
B vast
C varying
D vacuum

5 That speed is really great – ___
300,000 kilometres per second.
A appearing
B appeasing
C approximately
D approximation

6 This is what we mean when
we speak about the ___ .
A lightly
B speed of light
C speedy light
D light speeds

7 The electromagnetic ___
contains several kinds of waves.
A spectre
B spectrum
C spectacle
D spectacular

8 When they oscillate,
their ___ energy changes.
A cinema
B cinematic
C kinetic
D cordial

9 A large change in energy
produces ___ frequency radiation.
A highly
B higher
C height
D high

10 Radio waves are used
___ sound and pictures.
A to place
B emit
C to emit
D to transmit

11 Microwaves have a rather
large number of ___ .
A used ones
B usage
C uses
D useless

12 Continuous motion of ___
produces infrared waves.
A molecule
B molecular
C molecules
D molecularity

13 Infrared waves are mostly
___ by hot objects.
A given out
B given
C gave
D outnumbered

14 The infrared radiation ___
in the heat of an electric fire.
A is feeling
B feelings
C felt
D is felt

15 The wavelength of these
waves ___, you've learned that.
A vary
B very
C variable
D varies

16 Radio waves can be
of very low ___ .
A frequency
B frequent
C frequently
D freshly

17 It is interesting to know how
these waves ___ .
A are generated
B generated
C generate
D are ignored

18 To learn this, we first have
to know what ___ are.
A particular
B particle
C particularly
D particles

19 They produce the waves
when they change their ___ .
A energetically
B energetics
C energy
D energetic

20 Of course, they already
have a certain electrical ___ .
A change
B merge
C barge
D charge

21 This happens when an electron
changes ___ around a nucleus.
A orbiting
B all right
C biting
D orbit

22 It also happens when
electrons or___ oscillate.
A nuclei
B nuclear
C molecule
D atomic

23 Ultraviolet radiation is
a ___ of sunlight.
A component
B composer
C compose
D composed

24 It occurs ___ the violet end
of the visible light spectrum.
A behind
B beyond
C beneath
D belong

25 Remember to avoid an
___ of UV light! Be careful!
A size
B excess
C exercise
D exert

26 Yes, yes, all people know that!
UV light can be very ___ .
A harmed
B harm
C harmful
D harmless

27 However, much of the sun's UV
radiation is stopped by the ___ .
A ozone's
B ozone layer
C lying
D layers

28 Gamma rays are released
during radioactive ___ .
A disappear
B disturb
C decadence
D decay

29 We also know that gamma rays
are the most ___ of all radiations.
A penetrating
B periphery
C penetration
D performance

30 Ultraviolet radiation
is emitted by ___ objects.
A heat
B hotter
C white-hot
D heal

130

Test 22
DESKTOP PUBLISHING

1　The ___ standing for *desktop publishing* is DTP.
 A acquisition
 B application
 C abbreviate
 D abbreviation

2　DTP is the software and hardware that ___ the composition of text.
 A impossible
 B make possible
 C possibility
 D impossibility

3　The composition of text and ___ used to be done by printers only.
 A graphic
 B graphology
 C graphics
 D graphite

4　Desktop publishing ___ the use of a computer.
 A request
 B pebbles
 C recognize
 D requires

5　Also needed are a ___ printer and various software programs.
 A laser
 B lake
 C lasting
 D lash

6　It is possible to produce anything from a single ___ of text to ...
 A place
 B pace
 C page
 D pagination

7　This ___ publishing has been possible since the early 1970s.
 A computer aid
 B computer-aided
 C addition
 D added to computer

8　They can be sent to the printer ___ on the computer monitor.
 A as you saw
 B seen
 C always seen
 D as seen

9　Using this software many types of graphics can be ___ .
 A retold
 B portrayed
 C confused
 D created

10　The system may also ___ art and photographs from own sources.
 A incorporate
 B interpret
 C interfere
 D interference

11　Yes, art and photographs may be used from sources ___ the PC.
 A insidious
 B inserting
 C inside
 D initial

12　The command ___ for producing text and graphics are rather simple.
 A company's
 B codes
 C co-operate
 D colleagues

13　They are easy to learn because they really are ___ simple.
 A computer's
 B comparative
 C superlative
 D comparatively

14　Some computers use symbols and a ___ .
 A point
 B pointer
 C pointless
 D pointers

15 At first it was for organisations
willing ___ large sums of money.
A insect
B to investigate
C to invest
D investment

16 Traditional printers or ___
houses were such organisations.
A publishing
B published
C publishers
D publicly

17 DTP as ___ of PCs became
possible more than a decade later.
A functional
B functionality
C functioning
D a function

18 Indeed it became possible
on a ___ scale only in 1985.
A brothers'
B partial
C boarding
D broad

19 Print is produced by employing
a variety of ___ and type sizes.
A phonetics
B phone
C phones
D fonts

20 Typesetting ___ offered by DTP
software programs are numerous.
A capable
B able
C capabilities
D capacity

21 Page ___ are based on different
templates that are offered.
A laying
B lying
C lied
D layouts

22 They can be set up on the monitor
and ___ to the printer.
A transformed
B transferred
C translated
D transitory

23 The pointer is, of course,
___ by the mouse.
A connected
B compressed
C composed
D controlled

24 Some computers, on the other
side, use word and letter ___ .
A commands
B comments
C connects
D concern

25 You need to have a laser printer
able to print at 300 or more ___ .
A dates
B dots
C debts
D dots per inch

26 It goes without saying that a
word ___ software is necessary.
A processing
B playing
C staying
D helping

27 A separate program enables
the user to ___ blocks of type.
A manipulate
B positions
C manner
D module

28 Yes, I agree, 300 dpi provides
relatively low ___ .
A reserve
B solution
C resolution
D resolute

29 More complex laser printers
produce finer quality ___ .
A illustrations
B illustrated
C illustrating
D illustrative

30 A computer-connected ___ is
another fine addition.
A sequence
B device
C possibility
D scanner

Test 23
NUCLEAR ENERGY

1 Can you explain what ___
of radioactive elements is?

A acquired property
B controlled decay
C connected decision
D contracted task

2 Upon ___ , an element such as
uranium releases energy.

A deception
B determination
C decay
D destruction

3 The released energy is
___ which can be harnessed.

A hot
B hottest
C heat
D heal

4 The energy ___ per atom
is really difficult to imagine.

A gives
B given
C taken off
D given off

5 It is thousands of times more
plentiful than during ___ .

A burns
B burn
C lasting
D burning

6 The process often has to be
___ , however.

A afraid
B accelerated
C accepts
D again

7 This is done by ___
the material with neutrons.

A bombarding
B bombardment
C bombing
D bombed

8 Control rods serve
to control the ___ fission.

A statement of
B rate of
C stand on
D looking at

9 This all relates to
what they call a ___ reactor.

A representative
B thermostat
C thermal
D thermodynamics

10 Uranium-239 forms plutonium,
which ___ can be used as fuel.

A itself
B impersonal
C oneself
D interfere

11 Nuclear ___ has not yet been
harnessed for commercial purposes.

A fuse
B fusion
C fuses
D uses

12 Commercial purposes in the first
place include commercial ___ .

A powers
B powerful
C power used
D power production

13 It happens when two ___ are
combined to form a single nucleus.

A nucleus
B nuclear
C news
D nuclei

14 There, of course, is
an ___ release of energy.

A understood
B accompanying
C accompanied
D accepted

15 Nuclear fission is the
    ___ of radioactive atoms.
    A splitting
    B standing
    C starving
    D statement

16 It is the ___ in which electricity
    is generated from nuclear power.
    A want
    B why
    C way
    D weigh

17 In a nuclear ____ heat from the
    reactions heats water into steam.
    A road
    B ray
    C reactor
    D factor

18 This steam is then used
    ___ the turbines.
    A to ride
    B running
    C spending
    D to drive

19 The ___ of a reactor contains the
    nuclear fuel, e.g. uranium dioxide.
    A core
    B cone
    C cups
    D cart

20 Neutrons produced by
    the fission reactions are ___ .
    A slowly
    B slowing
    C slowed down
    D preserved

21 This is necessary to ensure
    the ___ reaction continues.
    A choose
    B chose
    C charm
    D chain

22 The energy released through such
    reaction becomes really ___ .
    A informative
    B humorous
    C translated
    D enormous

23 Nuclei ___ each other in case of
    the like electrical charge.
    A repel
    B reap
    C rasp
    D renew

24 This is why in this process
    very high ___ speeds are used.
    A comfortable
    B comment
    C complete
    D collision

25 This in practice means the use
    of ___ high temperatures.
    A invisibly
    B important
    C incredibly
    D implanted

26 Fusion occurs in the Sun
    in an ___ way.
    A unbelievably
    B uncontrolled
    C wonderfully
    D usefully

27 The ___ is in producing a lot of
    energy from a small amount of fuel.
    A benefits
    B benefit
    C benevolent
    D beverage

28 It does not produce gases
    that ___ to the greenhouse effect.
    A reserve
    B contribute
    C attribute
    D resolute

29 However, the ___ produced
    is extremely dangerous.
    A waist
    B wastes
    C waits
    D waste

30 It must be stored
    and ___ very carefully.
    A operated
    B devised
    C stayed
    D treated

Test 24
FACSIMILE TRANSMISSION

1   The word *fax* stands short
    for: ___ .
    A   *facsimile*
    B   *faculty*
    C   *faxing*
    D   *facultative*

2   It is a ___ capable of both
    transmitting or receiving.
    A   device
    B   deception
    C   decay
    D   devise

3   It transmits or receives ___
    copies of different materials.
    A   hot
    B   exactly
    C   exact
    D   exercises

4   The word is of pages of
    printed or ___ matter.
    A   pictures
    B   picturesque
    C   pictorial
    D   depicting

5   The pages are sent or received
    over ___ lines in less than 60 sec.
    A   telegraph
    B   television
    C   radio
    D   telephone

6   Some form of this has been ___
    since the end of the 19th century.
    A   available
    B   afterwards
    C   avalanche
    D   ability

7   Alexander Graham Bell's
    ___ was recognised in 1876.
    A   intended
    B   intention
    C   invention
    D   invitation

8   This ___ of standards
    is known as Group III.
    A   statement
    B   state
    C   set
    D   setting

9   These standards were
    ___ in 1980.
    A   implementation
    B   implanted
    C   implemented
    D   initiate

10 They require digital ___
    scanning, you know that.
    A   imagine
    B   imaginary
    C   image
    D   imaginative

11 These standards also
    require data ___ .
    A   compression
    B   compressor
    C   comprehensive
    D   comprise

12 *bps* stands short for:
    ___ per second.
    A   bitter
    B   bites
    C   bite
    D   bits

13 Machines ___ to conform to these
    standards transmit at 9,600 bps.
    A   build
    B   built
    C   bring
    D   bit

14 The original document
    is first ___ into the machine.
    A   feed
    B   feeding
    C   fled
    D   fed

15 A public service was ___
    three years later.
    A begun
    B began
    C begins
    D begin

16 It was after Bell ___ his
    invention to the United Kingdom.
    A has brought
    B have thought
    C had taught
    D had brought

17 It remained a relatively specialised
    ___ device for a long time.
    A communications
    B communicative
    C completing
    D communicated

18 Sophisticated scanning and ___
    techniques appeared much later.
    A digits
    B deletes
    C rigid
    D digitising

19 They appeared with new
    computer ___ .
    A technician
    B tectonic
    C technologies
    D technological

20 Special standards in this
    sphere also had to be ___ .
    A exported
    B imported
    C established
    D expected

21 Now fax machines communicate
    over ___ telephone lines.
    A ordinary
    B ordinates
    C co-ordinate
    D ordinarily

22 Most contemporary fax machines
    ___ to a set of standards.
    A confirm
    B connect
    C conform
    D conformity

23 In some faxes documents are
    scanned by a ___ of LEDs.
    A states
    B series
    C serial
    D slates

24 LED is an abbreviation for:
    light-emitting ___ .
    A decision
    B determinant
    C dual
    D diode

25 *Pixels*, or *pels* are light
    and dark *picture* ___ .
    A epochs
    B ellicit
    C elementary
    D elements

26 These light and dark
    elements are described ___ .
    A digital
    B digitally
    C digits
    D diagonally

27 The message is shortened
    by ___ much of the white space.
    A compressing
    B compressed
    C compasses
    D compression

28 The ___ machine is addressed
    through its telephone number.
    A reserved
    B reception
    C reciprocal
    D receiving

29 The ___ message is printed out
    on heat-sensitive paper.
    A reconstituted
    B recognition
    C refurbished
    D replied

30 Be careful! The heat-sensitive
    paper ___ over a period of time!
    A brown
    B borrows
    C betraying
    D browns

Test 25
THE RAYS THAT PENETRATE SOLID MATTER

1 X-rays are the rays that
penetrate ___ matter.
A sold
B solid
C solidarity
D solved

2 They are electromagnetic
waves with a ___ wavelength.
A short
B sharp
C shining
D solid

3 First, electrons moving at
high speed have to ___ a target.
A stroke
B struck
C strike
D striking

4 After that they are
___ very quickly.
A stared
B hoped
C stopped
D starting

5 These rays ___ in 1895
by Wilhelm Conrad Röntgen.
A discovered
B was discovered
C discoverer
D were discovered

6 He called this
___ radiation X-rays.
A unknown
B knowledge
C knowingly
D unkind

7 In fact X-rays were being emitted
as electrons ___ the anode.
A helped
B heat
C hit
D heal

8 They also make some
materials ___ .
A to fluoresce
B fluoresce
C fluorine
D floor

9 As already mentioned, these
rays ___ photographic film.
A effect
B in effect
C affectation
D affect

10 These ___ render X-rays
both useful and hazarduous.
A property
B popularity
C properties
D produced

11 Their ionisation effect
damages living ___ .
A tile
B ties
C tide
D tissue

12 By using very small doses,
they can be used ___ .
A for medicine
B medicinal
C medical
D in medicine

13 They can be used ___ X-ray
photographs of the body.
A to take
B taking
C took
D to make

14 The ___ to which the rays
are absorbed varies.
A explain
B expect
C extra
D extent

15 They hit the anode and the
walls of the cathode ray ___ .

A tube
B tubeless
C timber
D time

16 Atoms of all ___ give out
characteristic X-rays.

A elementary
B element
C elements
D primary

17 Electrons colliding with the
atom ___ electrons from inner orbitals.

A displace
B distinguish
C disrespect
D distasteful

18 Vacant places are then filled
by electrons from the ___ orbital.

A out
B older
C outing
D outer

19 These electrons ___ energy
as they move down.

A give
B give up
C given
D give out

20 X-rays have the ___ of
electromagnetic radiation.

A prepare
B prepared
C properties
D positions

21 They also penetrate solid
matter and ___ ionisation.

A cause
B case
C casing
D causal

22 Ionisation is produced by
___ of electrons from atoms.

A reference
B reform
C refined
D removal

23 It depends upon the ___ and the
atomic weight of the material.

A defense
B department
C dense
D density

24 The atomic weight is the ___
atomic mass of the material.

A relative
B relation
C replay
D relay

25 The lower these ___ , the more
easily will the rays penetrate.

A faculty
B frames
C facts
D factors

26 The flesh appears
___ in X-ray photographs.

A transparent
B transported
C traditional
D trading

27 The greater density of bone
makes bones appear ___ .

A ache
B opacity
C opaque
D stake

28 X-rays are used in industry
for checking ___ in metal.

A jaws
B jars
C points
D joints

29 X-ray crystallography is
an ___ tool in geology.

A alphabetical
B nautical
C analysis
D analytical

30 X-rays are also used in
industry for examining ___ .

A flights
B flows
C floods
D flaws

Test 26
ELECTRONS ACT AS MINUTE MAGNETS

1   Remember: electrons act
    as ___ magnets!
    A   mimimum
    B   minor
    C   minute
    D   minutes

2   Magnetism is the effective ___
    which originates within the Earth.
    A   forceful
    B   force
    C   fork
    D   forced

3   It behaves as if there were a ___
    magnet at the centre of the Earth.
    A   powerful
    B   powers
    C   powder
    D   paws

4   In this way a ___
    field is produced.
    A   magnetism
    B   magnet's
    C   magnify
    D   magnetic

5   The poles point approximately
    to the ___ north and south poles.
    A   discovery
    B   geography
    C   geology
    D   geographic

6   A ___ needle is a needle
    of freely swinging magnet.
    A   compass
    B   compasses
    C   competitive
    D   compassion

7   That needle will ___ itself
    along the line of the field.
    A   allow
    B   alone
    C   align
    D   alligned

8   Of course, iron does not
    ___ the magnetism.
    A   retain
    B   reflect
    C   restrain
    D   reform

9   This is why iron magnets
    are ___ magnets.
    A   temperature
    B   time
    C   table
    D   temporary

10 Steel magnets, on the other
    hand, are ___ magnets.
    A   propose
    B   popular
    C   permanent
    D   product

11 A way to produce a magnet is
    to slide a steel ___ into a solenoid.
    A   bark
    B   bar
    C   car
    D   place

12 A solenoid is a ___ through
    which current is passed.
    A   coil
    B   coincidence
    C   cone
    D   conical

13 Electromagnet is produced when
    magnetism is ___ in the steel.
    A   introduction
    B   induced
    C   injected
    D   implanted

14 In addition to iron, cobalt and
    nickel can also be ___ strongly.
    A   magnet
    B   magnify
    C   magnetised
    D   magnificent

15 In fact, the magnetic
    field ___ into the Earth.
    A dips
    B deep
    C deeply
    D depends

16 With the correct ___
    it can be seen easily.
    A instruct
    B instructor
    C instructor's
    D instrument

17 The magnetic field
    ___ towards the poles.
    A increase
    B inserts
    C increases
    D creases

18 A ___ magnet has
    north and a south pole.
    A ban
    B bar
    C bus
    D bed

19 The pole at the end ___ to the
    north is a north-seeking pole.
    A joining
    B points
    C proving
    D pointing

20 Iron ___ can easily
    be magnetised.
    A files
    B filings
    C fields
    D filled

21 Some materials can be
    magnetised ___ of a magnet.
    A in the presence
    B in presence
    C presented
    D in the present

22 Iron and ___ are examples
    of such materials.
    A stole
    B stealing
    C steal
    D steel

23 Materials that can be
    magnetised are called ___ .
    A ferrous
    B magnetic
    C magnets
    D ferro-magnetic

24 The materials called ___ are
    not affected by magnetism.
    A no metals
    B metallurgy
    C non-metals
    D metallic

25 Metals such as copper
    seem to be ___ by magnetism.
    A affectionate
    B unaffected
    C unimportant
    D interpreted

26 However, very strong magnets
    do show some ___ with them, too.
    A affect
    B affected
    C effectively
    D effect

27 Even today, the ___ of
    magnetism is unknown.
    A originate
    B origin
    C original
    D orbits

28 Magnetism is attributed
    to the flow of electric ___ .
    A curtain
    B court
    C connect
    D current

29 Electrons carry a ___ , and
    they act as minute magnets.
    A charge
    B chance
    C charcoal
    D character

30 They act as magnets as they
    ___ around their nuclei in atoms.
    A stand
    B splash
    C stay
    D spin

Test 27
MACHINES AND MECHANICS

1   *Machine* is basically a means of
    overcoming ___ at a point.

    A   resistance
    B   respect
    C   reserved
    D   restore

2   This is achieved by ___
    a force at another point.

    A   applauding
    B   applying
    C   application
    D   apparently

3   A machine does not ___
    the amount of work to be done.

    A   respectfully
    B   restriction
    C   reduce
    D   represents

4   It does, however, allow a work
    to be done more ___ .

    A   comparatively
    B   relatively
    C   conveniently
    D   obviously

5   There are six ___ *machines*
    in the study of physics.

    A   *served*
    B   *serving*
    C   *simple*
    D   *serious*

6   One of them is the
    so-called ___ *plane*.

    A   *imperative*
    B   *inclination*
    C   *indication*
    D   *inclined*

7   Each in its own way can be
    used for a ___ task.

    A   particular
    B   particle
    C   partly
    D   participation

8   When using the ramp, how
    can you ___ the *velocity ratio*?

    A   cabin
    B   calculate
    C   calculation
    D   calcium

9   It is essentially the ___ of the
    ramp over the height of the ramp.

    A   long
    B   longitude
    C   longing
    D   length

10 Have you heard of ___ ? It is
    an important part of physics.

    A   mechanic
    B   molecular
    C   mechanical
    D   mechanics

11 It deals with the way matter ___
    under the influence of forces.

    A   becomes
    B   boils
    C   brings
    D   behaves

12 In dynamics we deal with
    the changes of ___ .

    A   move
    B   motion
    C   motionless
    D   motives

13 Such changes result when
    objects are ___ to forces.

    A   subjected
    B   substituted
    C   described
    D   destroyed

14 *Kinematics* is the study of motion
    without ___ to mass.

    A   referee
    B   reference
    C   reverse
    D   refusal

15 The ___ is used when it is
necessary to raise a load.
A level
B lever
C law
D revolve

16 Everybody knows that
the wheel is used ___ a load.
A transporter
B as a transporter
C transporting
D to transport

17 More complex machines usually
involve the ___ of energy.
A impose
B input
C increases
D injection

18 The energy is needed for ___
a mechanism to achieve a task.
A deleting
B erasing
C counting
D driving

19 Qualities of a machine are its
mechanical ___ and *velocity ratio*.
A address
B advantage
C attribute
D atmosphere

20 A ___ does not appear
very much like a machine.
A *roar*
B *road*
C range
D *ramp*

21 It enables a load to be taken
gradually to a ___ .
A height
B high
C highly
D vertically

22 Some loads can simply
not be ___ vertically.
A lived
B left
C lifted
D lifting

23 In kinematics there is also
no attention paid to ___ .
A ferrous
B forceful
C forget
D force

24 It deals with ___ or acceleration
of parts of a moving system.
A velocity
B vocabulary
C vortex
D visual

25 Newton's law of motion
forms the ___ of mechanics.
A base
B basic
C bases
D basics

26 At the atomic level, behaviour is
explained by ___ *mechanics*.
A collective
B question
C quantity
D quantum

27 Machine basically serves
___ resistance at a point.
A to overcome
B overcoming
C coming over
D combining

28 At the atomic level,
different ___ are offered.
A explaining
B extreme
C explanations
D expecting

29 Do you find it ___ to explain
what velocity ratio is?
A different
B distant
C hardly
D difficult

30 Do you know ___ law of motion
we have to study now?
A whom
B whose
C why
D how

Test 28
DRIVER & APPLICATION INSTALLATION

1 Please read this driver *and* ___
installation instruction carefully.

A apply
B application
C appliance
D applicable

2 After you have ___ your PC,
start up this program.

A turned on
B turning on
C placed on
D turned up

3 Was this document ___ you
when you bought your PC?

A given
B gave
C offered
D given to

4 Have you ___ *Step 2*
of this Instruction?

A reading
B writing
C rode
D read

5 ___ after *Step 1* you will be
able to start the right thing.

A Shortly
B Shortened
C Short
D Certain

6 You will see the Found New
Hardware Wizard ___ box.

A direct
B dialog
C dialect
D detect

7 Insert the *Multimedia Software*
CD into your CD-ROM ___ .

A driver
B drives
C determination
D drive

8 Do you know what to do
if you see some ___ messages?

A warmth
B warning
C wearing
D wealth

9 If such messages ___ ,
please click *Continue Anyway*.

A show
B prepare
C show up
D slow

10 What do you have to do
after the installation ___ ?

A finished
B have finished
C finish
D is finished

11 Yes, you know you have
___ your computer!

A restart
B charge
C to restart
D change

12 Of course, you have chosen
to ___ your computer.

A boat
B boots
C repeat
D reboot

13 After this, the wizard will
___ install the new program.

A automation
B automatically
C absolutely
D afraid

14 Will this new ___
be installed quickly?

A apply
B apart
C application
D apartment

15 *Autorun* will start and
the menu ___ will appear.

A screw
B lever
C screen
D season

16 Next you have ___ the button
marked *TV Capture Card*.

A transport
B clicking
C cloning
D to click

17 The button marked like that
will appear on the virtual remote ___ .

A control
B contact
C controller
D contract

18 Now ___ the language
for the next step.

A choice
B chosen
C chose
D choose

19 The driver ___ is now
finally going to start.

A installation
B instruction
C inscription
D inspiration

20 Be patient and wait for
the ___ to instal the driver.

A wise
B why
C whisper
D wizard

21 A window will appear
___ the status.

A indicate
B indicating
C international
D injecting

22 Once again, you have to be
___ for a couple of minutes.

A point
B patient
C patent
D postponed

23 A box will appear ___ you
that the installation is finished.

A saying
B holding
C telling
D reminded

24 Please click *Yes* in
the next few steps ___ .

A to play
B continue
C complete
D to continue

25 Please click *OK* to finish
the ___ installation.

A entire
B entirely
C entrance
D basics

26 Have you read this
installation ___ carefully?

A guidance
B guides
C quantity
D guide

27 Do you find this installation
instruction easy to ___ ?

A do
B make
C follow
D found

28 During the installation,
a window shows the ___ .

A guides
B prospect
C explanation
D progress

29 After the computer ___
restarted, please click *OK*.

A had been
B was
C were
D has been

30 What happens when,
instead of *OK*, you click ___ ?

A Concept
B Cancel
C Council
D Contraction

Test 29
THE OZONE LAYER

1   What is the ozone ___ ?
    Have you ever heard of it?
    A   literature
    B   lays
    C   liar
    D   layer

2   Do you know what is ___
    to it currently?
    A   happened
    B   happens
    C   happening
    D   happy

3   It is higher than most
    aeroplanes ___ .
    A   flow
    B   flew
    C   fly
    D   flown

4   In fact it is between 15 and 40
    kilometres ___ the atmosphere.
    A   up in
    B   upon
    C   up
    D   into

5   This region ___ most of
    the atmosphere's ozone.
    A   connect
    B   contains
    C   container
    D   complains

6   Ozone is a special form
    of the gas ___ .
    A   oxygen
    B   oxide
    C   oxidize
    D   dioxide

7   Ozone has the ___ ability
    to stop certain dangerous rays.
    A   uniform
    B   unpleasant
    C   united
    D   unique

8   The ozone layer formed about
    two thousand ___ years ago.
    A   millions
    B   of millions
    C   million
    D   hundreds

9   At that time it was impossible
    ___ on the surface of the planet.
    A   to survive
    B   survival
    C   surrender
    D   survivor

10 This is exactly why all life
    was ___ in the oceans.
    A   deeply
    B   deep
    C   dip
    D   depend

11 Later, some of the oxygen
    in the air ___ ozone.
    A   turned
    B   turning
    C   returned
    D   turned to

12 Plants and animals could then
    begin to move on to ___ .
    A   sand
    B   land
    C   rock
    D   trend

13 Humans, however, are now ___
    the ozone layer for the first time.
    A   burning
    B   damaging
    C   learning
    D   having

14 This became obvious in
    the last couple of ___ .
    A   tens
    B   decade
    C   decisions
    D   decades

15 It stops certain dangerous
    ___ rays from the sun.
    A invisible
    B invented
    C information
    D intruders

16 It is very important to prevent
    such rays ___ the Earth's surface.
    A in taking
    B joining
    C from joining
    D from reaching

17 It is like a pair of sunglasses
    filtering ___ bright sunlight.
    A into
    B out
    C out of
    D connect

18 These rays are known
    as ___ radiation.
    A violet
    B infra
    C ultra-violet
    D ultra

19 This kind of radiation
    damages living ___ .
    A calls
    B cells
    C cellular
    D celestial

20 It also causes sunburn
    and more ___ diseases.
    A serene
    B seriously
    C serious
    D soul

21 This ozone is simply ___
    to life on the surface of the Earth.
    A very
    B vital
    C vitality
    D wanted

22 In other words, life on the
    surface of the Earth ___ it.
    A points
    B dependent
    C depends on
    D dependant

23 Now we know that some ___
    gases are destroying the ozone.
    A man-made
    B manly
    C made
    D foreign

24 They are used in everything,
    from refrigerators to fire ___ .
    A extinguish
    B distinguish
    C extinguishers
    D exercises

25 The most ___ of these gases
    are called chlorofluorocarbons.
    A certain
    B conclusion
    C basics
    D common

26 CFCs ___ short for the gases
    called chlorofluorocarbons.
    A plays
    B stays
    C stands
    D means

27 The damage produced to the
    ozone layer is ___ over Antarctica.
    A wore
    B worst
    C wearing
    D wound

28 Fortunately, natural ___ in the
    atmosphere create more ozone.
    A productions
    B product
    C processing
    D processes

29 Each year, however, it takes
    longer for the ___ to be completed.
    A healing
    B heard
    C prevailing
    D horizontal

30 All round the planet there now ___
    less ozone than even a few years ago.
    A seem
    B seems to be
    C seem to be
    D seemed

Test 30
NAVIGATION

1   What do we know about the ___
    of a vessel in the ancient times?
    A navigate
    B navigation
    C transportation
    D publication

2   It certainly depended on
    the ___ of the master.
    A experiment
    B experience
    C export
    D express

3   For every captain this work
    is really extremely ___ .
    A respect
    B responsibilities
    C reservations
    D responsible

4   For many centuries seamen had
    ___ on a knowledge of the coasts.
    A to repeat
    B rally
    C to rely
    D really

5   They also had to possess
    a knowledge of basic ___ .
    A astronomical
    B astronomer
    C astronomy
    D asteroid

6   Gradually various ___ were
    added to help the captain.
    A ads
    B adds
    C addition
    D aids

7   It was a long time before
    they left the ___ waters.
    A coastal
    B coasts
    C cost
    D cast

8   The new techniques ___
    near-perfect navigation.
    A proved
    B proffession of
    C provides
    D provided for

9   Despite the new techniques,
    ___ continued to be great.
    A risks
    B risky
    C hazarduous
    D connections

10 With excellent navigation
    techniques, ___ still occur today.
    A combination
    B collisions
    C connection
    D contradictory

11 Even today, fires
    ___ on powerful ships.
    A brake
    B breaks
    C breaking
    D break out

12 Isn't it surprising that even
    today many ships run ___ ?
    A ground
    B grind
    C grey
    D aground

13 Sinkings also cause loss of
    human life and valuable ___ .
    A wealthy
    B richess
    C possess
    D cargo

14 It is indeed surprising how
    ___ ships are lost every year.
    A much
    B many
    C more
    D too much

15 They finally ___ out
on to the open sea.
A ventured
B invented
C verified
D inspected

16 This means that proper sea
___ began only in Viking times.
A tournaments
B joints
C places
D voyages

17 Then came the discovery
of the ___ and hour glasses.
A connects
B compass
C to pass
D complete

18 This was followed by the
astrolabe, cross staff, the ___ .
A sextant
B express
C resultant
D instant

19 All of these were ___
to the voyages of discovery.
A certain
B cruising
C crucial
D cracked

20 Written navigation ___ seem to have
been possessed by the early sailors.
A instructors
B instructor
C inspiration
D instructions

21 In addition to these, ___ maps were
in use at the dawn of the New Age.
A impersonal
B impolite
C imperfect
D immediate

22 New ___ were developed in the
eighteenth and nineteenth centuries.
A technicians
B technology
C terrains
D techniques

23 Perfect communication is needed
between bridge and ___ .
A engines
B engine room
C engine
D cabins

24 In addition to telephone, there's the
automatic ___ of orders and data.
A transistor
B translate
C extinguisher
D transmission

25 The ___ and navigation equipment
of today is close to perfect.
A steering
B sterling
C standing
D outstanding

26 Yes, there are gyropilots, radars,
radiolocators, ___ systems, ...
A counter
B controller's
C reason
D remote-control

27 Accidents happen despite
the safety and watch ___ at sea.
A serve
B serving
C safes
D services

28 The power of the sea and
nature remains ___ , of course.
A production
B predictions
C processed
D unpredictable

29 Man has tried to ___ them for
over a thousand years now.
A mistake
B measures
C master
D ministers

30 Mistaken ___ of communications
data can also cause losses.
A evaluate
B evaluation
C elevation
D assassination

Test 31
THE MARTIANS ARE COMING!

1   I remember the days when
    the Martians were ___ earthward.

    A speed
    B speeding
    C spent
    D spending

2   The atomic ___ says that
    all things are made of atoms.

    A hypothesize
    B hypothesis
    C hypotheses
    D hyphen

3   Energy can only be ___
    from one form to another.

    A convert
    B converted
    C converting
    D converter

4   Lovers ___ in the parks
    with no thought of the danger.

    A wonder
    B wandered
    C wanders
    D wondered

5   Scientists know that
    such events are ___ .

    A prevention
    B preventable
    C to prevent
    D a prevention

6   The hot ___
    was like a meteorite.

    A cylinder
    B cylinder's
    C cylinders
    D cylindrical

7   Can you answer this simple
    question: What is ___ ?

    A meteors
    B meteorites
    C a meteorite
    D meteorological

8   I simply stood there,
    ___ with terror.

    A stricken
    B struck
    C strike
    D stroke

9   The two eyes were mirrors
    of an ___ brain.

    A extraordinary
    B mathematical
    C extra
    D mathematician's

10 They were cold, remorseless
    ___ unswayed by emotion.

    A intellectual
    B intelligence
    C intelligent
    D intelligences

11 The discovery of radioactivity
    has many practical ___ .

    A apply
    B application
    C applied
    D applications

12 The aicraft came within
    my ___ of vision.

    A range
    B running
    C road
    D ranch

13 Newton showed us the laws that
    govern how things ___ in the heavens.

    A motion
    B motivation
    C move
    D motionless

14 The wireless is really too noisy!
    Please ___ it down!

    A put
    B turn
    C gets
    D do

15   Revolvers, pistols, rifles and
     cannons are all types of ___ .
     A guns
     B gum
     C creates
     D fire

16   She was a wonderful singer,
     but illness has ___ her career.
     A blighted
     B bodies
     C spoil
     D prevent

17   What do we ___ about the
     constitution of matter?
     A knew
     B know
     C known
     D try

18   In what manner is engineering
     different from ___ ?
     A scientist
     B scientists
     C science
     D scientific

19   We were standing, and trucks
     ___ past us on the highway.
     A read
     B roared
     C stood
     D roaring

20   They were so afraid that
     they ___ about in the dark.
     A motion
     B moving
     C stumbled
     D standing

21   Do you know ___ mining and
     metallurgical engineering?
     A which are
     B where are
     C what is
     D why is

22   There was silence except for
     the ___ of traffic in the distance.
     A humble
     B hum
     C huge
     D heard

23   The Earth's location in the
     universe is unlikely to be ___ .
     A observation
     B inertia
     C motion
     D special

24   A ___ weight can do
     work in falling.
     A risen
     B rise
     C raise
     D raised

25   Is it possible to speak
     about the loss of ___ ?
     A energetics
     B energetic
     C energize
     D energy

26   The total ___ of energy in the
     universe remains constant.
     A month
     B amount
     C a month
     D monthly

27   A lot of ___ is also generated
     by nuclear reactions.
     A heating
     B reaction
     C hot
     D heat

28   The connection between electricity
     and ___ was revealed by Faraday.
     A magnetic
     B magnets
     C magnetism
     D the magnets

29   The monsters could slay with ___
     beyond the range of our biggest guns.
     A raid
     B heating
     C heat rays
     D recording

30   The old man remembers the dayswhen the
     Martians were speeding ___
     A Earth
     B Earth's
     C earthward
     D on Earth

Test 32
DAVID THE TEENAGE TYCOON

1   Teenager David Bolton
    has just put £9,000 ___ the bank.
    A   in
    B   at
    C   about
    D   of

2   He did that after only
    six months of ___ work.
    A   part-time
    B   show-time
    C   used to
    D   time

3   For six months he worked
    as a computer ___ .
    A   consultations
    B   consulate
    C   consultant
    D   consulting

4   That young boy is the ___ expert
    from Croydon, South London.
    A   electronical
    B   electrical
    C   electronics
    D   working

5   He is fast establishing a reputation
    as one of Britain's top ___ .
    A   troubles
    B   shooter
    C   troubleshooting
    D   troubleshooters

6   That young man is the person
    to call if no one else can ___ .
    A   hope
    B   cope
    C   core
    D   could

7   His first steps to fame and ___
    began when he was only nine.
    A   fortune
    B   found
    C   fortunately
    D   finally

8   Everything that happened to David
    came really ___ unexpectedly.
    A   complete
    B   quiet
    C   quite
    D   quietly

9   They gave him computers and
    ___ worth more than £3,000.
    A   soft
    B   software
    C   interested
    D   offered

10 In ___ , he has to send them
    a report every month.
    A   reason
    B   right
    C   true
    D   return

11 His reports say what he has done
    and ___ his plans are.
    A   which
    B   why
    C   whose
    D   what

12 David helps companies ___ which
    computers they should buy.
    A   by suggesting
    B   suggestion
    C   suggestions
    D   surprising

13 He also helps firms by writing
    ___ programs for them.
    A   individuals
    B   an individual
    C   individual's
    D   individual

14 Can you answer the simple question
    of ___ really motivates him?
    A   why
    B   where
    C   which
    D   what

15 His parents bought him
___ when he was still a kid.
A computing
B compute
C businesses
D a computer

16 He remembers that he learned ___
his machine when he was only nine.
A to program
B programmed
C a programme
D programming

17 He also remembers that he had
___ for ages to buy an Amstrad.
A save
B safety
C saving
D to save

18 After that he decided to get
serious about ___ .
A computer
B computer's
C a computer
D computing

19 He went to night school to learn
how to write ___ programs.
A businesses
B a business
C busy
D business

20 He also did a ___ course
with an American college.
A correspond
B correct
C correspondent
D correspondence

21 Later on he got in touch with
a computer ___ , Eltec.
A sale
B sell
C sales
D seller

22 They were so ___ that they
offered him a contract.
A impressive
B impressions
C impress
D impressed

23 This teenager can work more
quickly than many older ___ .
A places
B professions
C professionals
D professional

24 The problems that are reported
are to be ___ by the young genius.
A resolved
B solve
C solution
D solving

25 In one difficult case, David found the
problem and finished ___ in only five days!
A job
B doing
C the job
D work

26 In the short period he has been in
business David ___ about £9,000!
A has made
B have made
C have done
D has put

27 With that money he has bought
more ___ .
A to equip
B equipment
C a piece of equipment
D occupation

28 The question is: How
did he ___ it?
A does
B works
C do
D gets

29 You have to be ___ , and you have
to really want to get to the top!
A ambition
B aspiration
C ambitiousness
D ambitious

30 Believe in yourself, and ___yourself that
you're the best!
A tell
B say
C told
D said

Test 33
SOMETHING OUT OF STAR WARS?

1 No, that was really nothing
   out of Star ___ .
   A Wars
   B Warms
   C Warriors
   D Worried

2 This text was ___ in Time,
   on April 21, 1997.
   A publish
   B print
   C published
   D printing

3 It was also interesting to ask
   whether the sun ___ green.
   A turned
   B has turned
   C have turned
   D had turned

4 Have you ever thought
   that the sun ___ turn green?
   A must
   B needs
   C is capable of
   D could

5 Nobody ___ that,
   we are sure.
   A have thought
   B have ever thought
   C think
   D has ever thought

6 That glowing blob was
   actually a solar ___ .
   A pressure
   B appears
   C flame
   D flare

7 It hurtled ___ the Earth
   in mid April, 1997.
   A to
   B by
   C toward
   D at

8 They ___ from 6 hours to
   several days to pass Earth.
   A measures
   B take
   C make
   D go

9 The 1997 flare was ___
   after a 1989 one.
   A top
   B the largest
   C larger
   D bigger

10 The 1989 flare knocked ___
    a power grid in Quebec.
    A off
    B in
    C of
    D out

11 The power grid in Quebec
    ___ for nine hours.
    A knocked
    B was knocked off
    C was knocked out
    D knocked out

12 Flares can disturb
    the Earth's ___ field.
    A magnets
    B magnet
    C magnesium
    D magnetic

13 Flares can also give heart
    attacks to telephone ___ .
    A link
    B line
    C lines
    D lined

14 Electronic ___ can also be
    seriously affected.
    A transmit
    B transmissions
    C transmitted
    D perform

15 The phenomenon ___
    on camera by NASA's SOHO.
    A catch
    B was caught
    C were caught
    D to catch

16 The camera was carried by
    NASA's SOHO ___ .
    A crafts
    B space
    C spaces
    D spacecraft

17 The sun virtually
    ___ out the flare.
    A spit
    B spitting
    C spot
    D spat

18 The flare consisted of ___
    charged hydrogen and helium.
    A ton
    B tons of
    C tons off
    D a ton

19 The sun ___ it toward Earth
    at about .2.4 million kph.
    A propelled
    B propel
    C propeller
    D proposed

20 *kph* stands for:
    kilometres per ___ .
    A hours
    B house
    C hour
    D how

21 Flares normally ___
    every three or four years.
    A occur
    B OK
    C occurs
    D has occured

22 They usually stretch ___
    50 million kilometres.
    A after
    B across
    C a cross
    D immediately

23 They really take up to
    several days ___ Earth.
    A to pass
    B passed
    C having passed
    D has passed

24 Earthlings, however,
    need not ___ .
    A fear
    B fright
    C fearful
    D frightening

25 Scientists say that such
    flares are ___ to humans.
    A harm
    B harmless
    C less
    D difficult

26 The few common effects are
    limited to ___ telephone calls.
    A mist
    B misty
    C missed
    D misuse

27 Maybe this can make
    people ___ again.
    A reading
    B reader
    C has read
    D read

28 A flare-watcher in New York
    hoped that people ___ again.
    A will read
    B was reading
    C reading
    D would read

29 Flares also set ___
    pretty auroras.
    A away
    B off
    C of
    D from

30 Have you ever seen the
    phenomenon of the ___ ?
    A Northern
    B North
    C Lights
    D Northern Lights

Test 34
ARCTIC OBSESSION REMAINS RELEVANT

1   The Arctic is certainly one of the
___ environments on Earth.
A   hospitality
B   most hostile
C   host
D   hostess

2   Advenure, failure and ___ are
most often connected with it.
A   disastrous
B   discourage
C   disintegrate
D   disaster

3   The subjects ___ in an exhibition
at the National Maritime Museum.
A   are tackled
B   touched
C   touch
D   are played

4   It is organised with the aim of bringing
British ___ of the Arctic to life.
A   explanation
B   expenditure
C   exploration
D   expansion

5   The exhibition ___ the many
failed and disastrous expeditions.
A   concentrate
B   concrete
C   compensates
D   concentrates on

6   Those explorers were keen to
discover and ___ the passage.
A   connect
B   state
C   continue
D   map

7   They believed it would act as a
___ between Europe and the East.
A   trade
B   trade route
C   freight
D   trade name

8   There we are offered stark
illustrations of Arctic survival ___ .
A   technological
B   techniques
C   tectonic
D   technician

9   There are many interesting
artefacts ___ .
A   display
B   displaying
C   distribution
D   on display

10 Also ___ will be drawings
from John Ross' 1829 voyage.
A   on show
B   were shown
C   showing
D   showcase

11 These drawings ___ the first
encounter with the native Inuits.
A   documentary
B   a documentary
C   document
D   documents

12 The magnetic north pole
was ___ in 1831.
A   discovered
B   constructed
C   invented
D   prepared

13 We can see now the original flag
___ which was used to mark it.
A   staple
B   big
C   fast
D   staff

14 Would you ever like
to join their ___ ?
A   apart
B   adventure
C   again
D   advertise

15 The exhibition is not just a
nostalgic stroll ___ history.

A resulting
B in
C that
D through

16 It is intended to ___ important
environmental and political issues.

A rise
B evident
C rose
D raise

17 Mr. Rubenstein is the
spokesman ___ the museum.

A in
B of
C from
D for

18 They are currently measuring
the ___ of the ice in the region.

A thickness
B thick
C dense
D dance

19 Yes, we are having a strong
___ on the region's wildlife.

A important
B impact
C impersonal
D impolite

20 The whole world is once again
___ on the Arctic region.

A discussing
B focussing
C forbidden
D further

21 We also know that there are
significant oil ___ in the area.

A deploy
B determination
C deposits
D discover

22 Have you heard of Sir John
Franklin's ___ voyage in 1845?

A dim
B dome
C doomed
D dominant

23 There are more than objects
– maps, letters, ___ , paintings, ...

A draught
B drawing
C carving
D drawings

24 This exhibition means their hope
to bring exploration of the Arctic ___ .

A to life
B living
C lived
D into the life

25 Various questions are expected
to be provoked in the minds of ___ .

A visits
B visitors
C vital
D complexity

26 The exhibition is certainly
___ by environmental issues.

A moved
B motives
C motivated
D motivation

27 This trade route leading to the
East was hoped to be a ___ one.

A lived
B restrict
C not losing
D lucrative

28 The exhibition is set ___ at the
National Museum next month.

A opening
B to open
C opened
D open

29 The native Inuit artefacts to be
seen there are from ___ century.

A nine
B nineteenth
C nineteen
D the nineteenth

30 The Arctic obsession seems
to remain ___ , doesn't it?

A relief
B revive
C relieved
D relevant

Test 35
WHO EXACTLY ARE THE POOR PEOPLE OF THE WORLD?

1 Who ___ are the poor people
of the world?
A effect
B in effect
C exact
D exactly

2 Some ___ groups are more
likely to be poor than others.
A socialist
B socially
C social
D society

3 If you are ___ , for example, you
are much more likely to be poor.
A newcomer
B a refugee
C refused
D a refusal

4 The same is true for the ___ in the
USA, or the Aborigines in Australia.
A Native Americans
B new America
C nation
D American

5 The big question we need to answer
is: Why does ___ exist?
A poverty
B poor
C pour
D poorly

6 Why are some countries
so much ___ than others?
A poor
B poorer
C poorest
D power

7 There are many possible
___ of poverty.
A cause
B collisions
C case
D causes

8 Some countries ___ industrial
development in the past.
A experienced
B inexperienced
C experience
D expired

9 Their own industrial ___
made such countries richer.
A grows
B growth
C grew
D grown up

10 Many other countries ___
by the industrial nations.
A explicit
B were expected
C explored
D were exploited

11 Such countries ___
poor even today.
A restless
B reform
C remind
D remain

12 They had to ___ from
the developed countries.
A lend
B rent
C let
D borrow

13 They still owe huge amounts
of money in foreign ___ .
A doubt
B debt
C indebted
D debtors

14 One final cause of poverty
is certainly ___ .
A policy
B police
C polite
D politics

15 A country may be poor
simply ___ its location.
A owing to
B owed to
C owed
D owns

16 If you are old, again you
are much ___ to be poor.
A liked
B liking
C more likely
D more lovingly

17 Areas with poor ___
are usually poor ones.
A sale
B salt
C soil
D coil

18 Areas with bad ___ are
also rather poor ones.
A climates
B climatic
C climate
D climbing

19 Environment, of course,
is ___ this.
A relative
B related to
C relatives to
D relations

20 Poor countries are usually the
ones that ___ natural disasters.
A suffered
B suffer from
C suffering from
D surfers

21 When we say disasters we mean,
___ , hurricanes and floods.
A instance
B instantly
C for instance
D institute

22 There are also ___
reasons for poverty.
A historical
B history
C prehistoric
D historians

23 Countries which are ___
politically tend to be poorer.
A solution
B unstable
C stable
D resolved

24 Poor are the countries which
have suffered war or ___ .
A civilians
B civil war
C warriors
D waging

25 The poverty trap
is always worth ___ .
A mentioning
B mentioned
C minded
D to mention

26 This is what we might call
the ___ circle of poverty.
A vital
B vicious
C vice
D vicinity

27 This is very important
at a ___ level.
A person's
B person
C personnel
D personal

28 Many poor children in the world
never get a good ___ .
A competitive
B educational
C education
D compete

29 The worst jobs pay
very low ___ .
A wages
B wage
C waggons
D wagers

30 Poor people have very little
money ___ their children.
A bring
B bring up
C to bring up
D bringing up

158

Test 36
SINGING SANDS AND BOOMING DUNES

1 Have you heard of ___ sands
and booming dunes in California?
A singing
B sang
C singer
D saw

2 Some features of the California
environment are ___ natural.
A questioned
B questions
C unquestionably
D to be questioned

3 However, this does not
___ their mystery or allure.
A diminish
B detect
C deform
D depart

4 There are, for example,
sand ___ that sing!
A domes
B dunes
C duties
D duration

5 There are also stones that ___
across the parched desert floor.
A ride
B roaring
C race
D raced

6 Briny waves can sometimes sound
like the ___ of distant drums.
A boring
B beeping
C buying
D beating

7 These may all be natural___
of the California landscape.
A preferences
B procedures
C occupations
D occurences

8 The sand grains also
have ___ silica.
A connect
B to contain
C to complete
D complain

9 A certain stable ___
must be present , too.
A humidify
B humidifiers
C humid
D humidity

10 This, of course, ___
the size of the grains.
A depend
B depends on
C pending
D comprehend

11 The ___ the material
has travelled, the better.
A farther
B farthest
C far
D so far

12 As a result of wind, the individual
grains are usually more ___ .
A united
B uncertain
C uniform
D unfortunate

13 The landscape of Kelso Dunes
is ___ SoCal desert.
A type
B types
C typed
D typical

14 If you do not know what SoCal
___ , try to make a logical guess!
A stood
B stands for
C waits for
D looks at

15 They evoke strange ___ in those who experience them.
A senses
B sensible
C sentimental
D sensations

16 These anomalies can perhaps be taken as unnatural ___ .
A wonderful
B wanders
C wonders
D wandered

17 Seven places in the ___ US are home to the singing sands.
A continent
B concerted
C continental
D completed

18 Mojave Desert is a home to the singing-sand ___ .
A connects
B concerts
C concludes
D complicate

19 Remember! The only way in is ___ .
A hike
B hiking
C to hike
D hiding

20 There you can hear the plain old sand ___ unearthly sounds.
A radiating
B erasing
C emission
D emitting

21 For this to occur, several exacting ___ need to be present.
A factories
B fractions
C fact
D factors

22 The grains have to be between 0.1 and 0.5 millimeters ___ .
A in diameter
B diagonal
C radius
D arc

23 There the usual desert scrub stretches to the ___ .
A horizontal
B horizontally
C vertically
D horizon

24 The main sand hill is six ___ and fifty feet high.
A tens
B hundreds
C thousands
D hundred

25 That main sand hill is ___ from the road.
A vision
B visual
C vista
D visible

26 There are a few ___ to get the sand to perform.
A meetings
B methods
C methodology
D meaning

27 *Go to the top!* would probably be the best ___ .
A institution
B instructor
C insider
D instruction

28 Go to the top, and kick sand down the ___ side!
A slow
B step
C steep
D steeple

29 For this to achieve, ___ sure the day is calm.
A obtain
B supply
C remains
D make

30 Unstable ___ keep the sand cascading evenly.
A causes
B cases
C conditions
D conditional

Test 37
SO HANG ON TIGHT, FOLKS!

1   Start doing this test and
    – hang on ___ , folks!
    A tightly
    B tight
    C tighten
    D flight

2   At that moment the forward
    cabin door slammed ___ .
    A close
    B closer
    C clause
    D closed

3   A few moments later
    the aircraft began ___ .
    A motion
    B moved
    C moving
    D motionless

4   The Captain and the ___
    wished them a pleasant flight.
    A crowd
    B crew
    C crewed
    D screw

5   More essential were the
    ___ about emergency exits.
    A announcements
    B advertise
    C advert
    D announcers

6   Passengers have to know
    how to use their ___ masks.
    A oxide
    B oxygen
    C ex
    D extras

7   Stewardesses ___
    how to use these masks.
    A demonstration
    B demonstrating
    C demonstrate
    D demonstrative

8   You should know that
    this is ___ normal.
    A pure
    B perfection
    C perfectly
    D purification

9   It is done as a ___ to those
    who live near the airport.
    A courtesy
    B courtyard
    C contract
    D court

10 She knew that the second
    statement was a ___ .
    A lie
    B lay
    C lying
    D lies

11 The power reduction was
    neither normal nor ___ .
    A desirable
    B desire
    C decision
    D destroyable

12 The truth was: it was a
    ___ relations gesture.
    A politely
    B publicity
    C publication
    D public

13 It really involved
    ___ to aircraft safety.
    A risky
    B risk
    C risking
    D full of risk

14 Many pilots refused
    ___ power restrictions.
    A observe
    B observations
    C to observe
    D preserve

15 The plane was now
ready ___ .
A for taking
B to take after
C to take off
D took off

16 She noticed that everything
went ___ than usual.
A slow
B more slowly
C slowed
D slightly

17 It took them longer than usual
to reach their takeoff ___ .
A runway
B run away
C running away
D runner

18 No doubt the reason was
___ and the storm.
A lights
B signal
C traffic
D patrol

19 There was one more
announcement ___ .
A make
B to be made
C having made
D had made

20 It was required at
airports with ___ nearby.
A resident
B residential areas
C areas
D residents

21 You will notice a marked
___ in engine noise!
A crease
B crisis
C decrease
D subscribe

22 Don't worry! It is
due to a ___ in power.
A residence
B subtraction
C attraction
D reduction

23 They refused them
at risk of their ___ .
A careers
B careless
C carriers
D carefree

24 From a window Gwen could
see the lights of ___ aircraft.
A each other
B others
C other than
D another

25 She could also see
several ___ in line behind.
A other
B another
C one another
D others

26 The ___ ahead was turning on
to a runway.
A that
B ones
C one
D oneself

27 At that moment Gwen
___ down a folding seat.
A pushing
B pulled
C possessed
D forcing

28 After that she
___ herself in.
A stripes
B striped
C strapped
D trapping

29 The other girls
had found seats ___ .
A else
B or else
C elsewhere
D well as

30 The beginning of the ___
brought her the sense of relief.
A fly
B flying
C flew
D flight

Test 38
THE SECRET OF DR NO

1   The two men didn't
    talk ___ .
    A to each other
    B each other
    C one another
    D one other

2   There was no nervous ___
    about how tired they were.
    A chase
    B chatter
    C clatter
    D chapter

3   They just drove the machine
    quietly and ___ along.
    A effective
    B effect
    C in effect
    D efficiently

4   They were about to finish
    their ___ job.
    A completed
    B competent
    C complexity
    D complicate

5   Bond still had no idea
    what this ___ was.
    A competence
    B contraption
    C machines
    D mechanical

6   Under the black and gold paint
    it was some sort of ___ .
    A traction
    B tractor
    C a tractor
    D contraction

7   It was certainly of a kind
    he had never seen or ___ .
    A listened
    B heard
    C heard of
    D hearing

8   It had been added to help
    the dragon ___ .
    A fact
    B factor
    C defect
    D effect

9   It was obvious that the high
    mudguards had been ___ .
    A extension
    B extracted
    C exact
    D extended

10 They were given the shape
    of short ___ wings.
    A backswept
    B backing
    C sweeping back
    D swaying back

11 A long metal dragon's head
    had been added to ___ .
    A the front
    B front
    C a frontal
    D in front of

12 In fact it had been added
    to the ___ .
    A radiate
    B radiation
    C radiator
    D radioactive

13 The ___ had been given
    black centres.
    A head
    B limp
    C lamp
    D headlamps

14 The cabin had been covered
    with an armoured ___ .
    A dam
    B dome
    C dummy
    D demo

15 The wheels had their
    vast rubber ___ .
    A tired
    B tiresome
    C tireless
    D tyres

16 They were nearly
    ___ as tall as himself.
    A two
    B twofold
    C twelve
    D twice

17 He could see no
    trade ___ on them.
    A place
    B nickname
    C surname
    D name

18 It was too dark, but he
    could see they were ___ .
    A lights
    B solid
    C soldier
    D solidarity

19 They were perhaps
    filled with ___ rubber.
    A portion
    B pores
    C porous
    D porosity

20 At the ___ there was
    a small trailing wheel.
    A rare
    B rarely
    C roar
    D rear

21 Yes, that was a small
    trailing wheel for ___ .
    A stable
    B stability
    C stabilize
    D stabilization

22 An iron ___ , painted black
    and gold, had been added.
    A fine
    B finer
    C final
    D fin

23 There was a flame
    ___ mounted there.
    A threw
    B thrower
    C throwing
    D thorough

24 But – why that, instead of
    a ___ gun?
    A mechanical
    B merchant
    C mechanic
    D machine

25 It was the only sort of ___
    that could travel the island.
    A vehicle
    B vehement
    C velocity
    D whisper

26 The huge wheels would
    ride across the ___ lake.
    A solid
    B shallow
    C sharp
    D stubborn

27 At night, the ___ in the iron
    cabin would remain tolerable.
    A hot
    B hottest
    C host
    D heat

28 The truth is he was always
    impressed by ___ .
    A professional
    B profession
    C professionalism
    D professionally

29 He wouldn't be allowed
    to ___ with his knowledge.
    A get on
    B get away
    C stay put
    D get across

30 Could he prove her innocence
    and have her ___ ?
    A spoken
    B stayed
    C remained
    D spared

Test 39
ITALY HIT BY QUAKE TERROR

1   Early in April, 2009, Italy
    was ___ by quake terror.
    A hoped
    B hold
    C kick
    D hit

2   It was Italy's ___ earthquake
    for almost three decades.
    A disastrous
    B deadliest
    C deadly
    D disaster

3   The quake ___ 26 towns
    and villages in a few seconds.
    A destroyed
    B touching
    C touch
    D placed

4   Unfortunately at least 91 ___
    were killed and 1,500 injured.
    A person
    B man
    C peoples
    D people

5   Early in the morning,
    at 3.30am, most were ___ .
    A asleep
    B dream
    C sleep
    D slope

6   A lady said that she woke up
    hearing what ___ like a bomb.
    A connected
    B sounds
    C played
    D sounded

7   Really – everything was
    ___ , furniture falling...
    A trading
    B shook
    C shaking
    D standing

8   A ___ said that it was
    a true catastrophe.
    A sovereignty
    B technique
    C survivor
    D surfing

9   He managed to get to a
    ___ camp with his family.
    A relieve
    B relieved
    C relief
    D relative

10 The quake started in the ___
    Appennine region of Abruzzo.
    A centre
    B circle
    C centered
    D central

11 The epicentre was ___ to
    L'Aquila, a city of 70,000.
    A close
    B near
    C vicinity
    D by

12 ___ damaged buildings
    up to 100km (60 miles) away.
    A Tremors
    B Rumours
    C Street
    D Trades

13 Some towns in the area
    were ___ destroyed.
    A very
    B virtue
    C virtual
    D virtually

14 Yes, really, they were
    destroyed in their ___ .
    A entire
    B enough
    C entirety
    D entirely

15 The country's Prime Minister
soon ___ a state of emergency.
A declared
B defended
C destroyed
D determined

16 He did that when it was clear that
50,000 people had been left ___ .
A homeless
B evident
C home
D without

17 Another 100,000 people
___ the quake-hit zone.
A flee
B flow
C flew
D fled

18 ___ said that the situation
was worse than serious.
A Officials
B Officer
C Officially
D Offer

19 Even L'Aquila's main
hospital had to be ___ .
A leave
B lived
C transported
D evacuated

20 They left the building as
it really could ___ .
A destroy
B frame
C forbid
D collapse

21 We also know that all
sorts of other fears ___ .
A mountain
B determined
C hills
D mounted

22 The rescue operation was
___ by blocked roads.
A hurry
B done
C doom
D hampered

23 Even the metre-thick walls
of Mr. Peacock's house ___ .
A drew
B threw
C shook
D shock

24 It felt like the house was
being ___ from the rooftop.
A shake
B shaken
C shook
D shaking

25 He remembered that his bed was
___ against the wall all the time.
A banged
B banging
C hanging
D played

26 In addition, he could also
hear ___ all that time.
A creaking
B playing
C running
D standing

27 That shaking ___
for twenty seconds or so.
A go on
B went on
C going out
D went out

28 He said that the earth
really felt like jelly ___ .
A underneath
B under
C undergo
D understand

29 The European Union
immediately offered Italy ___ .
A aided
B added
C ads
D aid

30 Italy has not been hit by
a quake of such ___ since 1980.
A power
B powerful
C mighty
D force

AROUND THE WORLD IN 46 DAYS ... BY ALBATROSS

1 An albatross is really
   a majestic ___ , isn't it?
   A creative
   B create
   C crater
   D creature

2 Its ___ have always been
   shrouded in mystery.
   A movements
   B medals
   C motion
   D motionless

3 Scientists have recently made a
   great ___ about this mighty bird.
   A discoverer
   B discovery
   C distant
   D discipline

4 An albatross can fly ___ the
   world in just forty-six days!
   A about
   B after
   C around
   D afraid

5 Until now ___ has been known
   about the world's largest bird.
   A small
   B many
   C tiny
   D little

6 A study has revealed that
   it likes incredibly long ___ .
   A voyage
   B trips
   C speeds
   D journeys

7 The birds were studied by a team
   from the British Antarctic ___ .
   A Surface
   B Suggest
   C Stay
   D Survey

8 Do you know where they go during
   the months between breeding ___ ?
   A seasons
   B seasonal
   C season
   D seasonally

9 This study has been the first to
   show how they ___ that time.
   A spend
   B risky
   C concentrate
   D spending

10 Scientists attached ___ devices
    to the legs of albatrosses.
    A tractor
    B traction
    C tracking
    D trolley

11 An albatross lives most of
    its life (85 per cent) ___ sea.
    A at
    B on
    C in
    D under

12 Albatrossess have always
    been known as expert ___ .
    A swimmers
    B grinders
    C runners
    D gliders

13 They can sleep in the air,
    while ___ at 25mph!
    A connecting
    B cruising
    C containing
    D carrying

14 Have you known about
    the ___ in their beaks?
    A tales
    B tails
    C tune
    D tubes

15 Three of the studied birds ___ the globe twice.
A contained
B invested
C circumference
D circumnavigated

16 One of the birds ___ the 13,750-mile journey in 46 days!
A toured
B joined
C master
D managed

17 The ___ hope these data will prove useful.
A expert
B professor
C research
D researchers

18 In fact they hope their ___ will help other scientists.
A findings
B founded
C invented
D discovered

19 This will hopefully help ___ the unnecessary slaying of the birds.
A reproduce
B reduce
C receive
D reception

20 Many die each year after becoming ___ on fishing hooks.
A taught
B cough
C thought
D caught

21 This interesting ___ was published in the journal *Science*.
A student
B state
C study
D studies

22 Albatross has been part of ___ mythology for centuries.
A master
B maritime
C sailor's
D sailing

23 These tubes strain out ___ salt from water.
A success
B excessive
C exercise
D access

24 There are about twenty different ___ of albatross.
A special
B specialists
C species
D specify

25 Outstanding among these is the so-called ___ albatross.
A wonderful
B wandering
C wanders
D wonders

26 This albatross definitely has the widest ___ .
A window
B winged
C winner
D wingspan

27 ___ have shown albatrosses can live to the age of eighty!
A Records
B Recorder
C Camcorder
D Recording

28 However, ___ it is no longer than about thirty-five.
A average
B drainage
C averages
D on average

29 I've recently learned that their name ___ back to the 15th century.
A data
B date
C dates
D datum

30 We've also learned that *alcatraz* is the ___ word for *large seabird*.
A Portugal
B Porto
C portion
D Portuguese

KLJUČ

- REŠENJA TESTOVA -

TEST 1

1b	2a	3b	4c	5b	6d	7c	8b	9c	10d
11d	12a	13b	14b	15a	16a	17d	18c	19a	20a
21d	22c	23d	24d	25b	26d	27a	28c	29b	30a

TEST 2

1b	2c	3a	4c	5b	6a	7a	8c	9b	10a
11d	12c	13a	14c	15a	16b	17b	18b	19c	20a
21c	22d	23d	24b	25a	26b	27d	28d	29c	30d

TEST 3

1c	2a	3b	4c	5a	6d	7a	8a	9b	10d
11d	12d	13b	14c	15c	16c	17c	18d	19a	20a
21b	22a	23d	24a	25c	26b	27b	28d	29a	30a

TEST 4

1c	2d	3b	4a	5a	6b	7d	8a	9d	10b
11b	12d	13b	14d	15d	16b	17d	18b	19a	20d
21c	22c	23c	24b	25d	26b	27a	28b	29d	30c

TEST 5

1c	2a	3a	4b	5d	6c	7b	8a	9b	10c
11d	12d	13d	14d	15a	16d	17b	18b	19d	20c
21b	22a	23a	24d	25b	26c	27a	28b	29c	30a

170

TEST 6

1a	2b	3d	4c	5c	6a	7d	8b	9c	10b
11b	12b	13d	14b	15b	16b	17b	18a	19d	20b
21c	22b	23b	24d	25a	26c	27d	28b	29b	30d

TEST 7

1b	2d	3a	4a	5c	6d	7a	8a	9d	10c
11b	12b	13d	14b	15c	16a	17b	18a	19d	20d
21a	22b	23d	24d	25c	26a	27d	28d	29a	30c

TEST 8

1d	2c	3b	4a	5d	6b	7a	8d	9b	10c
11a	12d	13a	14d	15c	16d	17b	18d	19b	20a
21d	22a	23c	24c	25a	26a	27d	28b	29b	30c

TEST 9

1c	2d	3a	4d	5a	6c	7b	8a	9a	10c
11d	12c	13b	14b	15d	16d	17b	18c	19c	20b
21a	22d	23b	24b	25c	26a	27d	28d	29d	30b

TEST 10

1b	2d	3d	4a	5d	6b	7a	8d	9b	10a
11d	12d	13c	14a	15a	16a	17c	18b	19b	20d
21a	22a	23d	24b	25d	26d	27d	28d	29c	30a

TEST 11

1d	2d	3c	4b	5b	6b	7d	8d	9b	10d
11d	12a	13b	14a	15c	16b	17a	18c	19b	20b
21a	22d	23c	24a	25d	26d	27c	28d	29d	30b

TEST 12

1d	2d	3d	4c	5c	6c	7d	8b	9d	10d
11a	12a	13d	14a	15d	16c	17b	18b	19b	20b
21c	22d	23c	24c	25a	26d	27b	28d	29b	30b

TEST 13

1a	2b	3c	4c	5c	6b	7a	8b	9d	10a
11d	12a	13b	14d	15d	16d	17c	18d	19a	20d
21b	22d	23d	24c	25d	26a	27d	28c	29b	30d

TEST 14

1d	2a	3b	4d	5c	6d	7a	8b	9c	10c
11c	12b	13c	14d	15d	16d	17b	18b	19b	20d
21c	22d	23b	24a	25b	26c	27b	28b	29d	30b

TEST 15

1c	2d	3c	4b	5d	6b	7b	8b	9a	10a
11d	12b	13d	14d	15c	16a	17a	18c	19c	20a
21b	22d	23b	24d	25a	26c	27d	28d	29c	30b

TEST 16

1d	2c	3b	4d	5b	6a	7d	8c	9d	10d
11c	12c	13b	14a	15b	16d	17b	18d	19c	20d
21a	22d	23d	24d	25c	26b	27d	28a	29c	30d

TEST 17

1b	2a	3d	4b	5c	6b	7b	8a	9b	10a
11d	12d	13d	14b	15d	16b	17a	18d	19c	20b
21a	22b	23d	24d	25c	26d	27a	28d	29c	30b

TEST 18

1a	2b	3a	4b	5a	6a	7c	8a	9a	10c
11a	12b	13d	14a	15b	16b	17a	18b	19b	20d
21a	22a	23a	24c	25d	26b	27d	28c	29a	30c

TEST 19

1d	2a	3c	4b	5a	6c	7d	8b	9c	10b
11d	12d	13a	14b	15d	16d	17b	18d	19d	20c
21d	22c	23b	24a	25d	26c	27d	28b	29b	30d

TEST 20

1a	2b	3d	4c	5b	6b	7d	8c	9a	10b
11c	12d	13c	14b	15d	16d	17b	18a	19b	20c
21d	22c	23d	24b	25d	26c	27b	28a	29d	30a

TEST 21

1b	2b	3a	4d	5c	6b	7b	8c	9d	10d
11c	12c	13a	14d	15d	16a	17a	18d	19c	20d
21d	22a	23a	24b	25b	26c	27b	28d	29a	30c

TEST 22

1d	2b	3c	4d	5a	6c	7b	8d	9d	10a
11c	12b	13d	14b	15c	16a	17d	18d	19d	20c
21d	22b	23d	24a	25d	26a	27a	28c	29a	30d

TEST 23

1b	2c	3c	4d	5d	6b	7a	8b	9c	10a
11b	12d	13d	14b	15a	16c	17c	18d	19a	20c
21d	22d	23a	24d	25c	26b	27b	28b	29d	30d

TEST 24

1a	2a	3c	4c	5d	6a	7c	8c	9c	10c
11a	12d	13b	14d	15a	16d	17a	18d	19c	20c
21a	22c	23b	24d	25d	26b	27a	28d	29a	30d

TEST 25

1b	2a	3c	4c	5d	6a	7c	8b	9d	10c
11d	12d	13a	14d	15a	16c	17a	18d	19d	20c
21a	22d	23d	24a	25d	26a	27c	28d	29d	30d

TEST 26

1c	2b	3a	4d	5d	6a	7c	8a	9d	10c
11b	12a	13b	14c	15a	16d	17c	18b	19d	20b
21a	22d	23d	24c	25b	26d	27b	28d	29a	30d

TEST 27

1a	2b	3c	4c	5c	6d	7a	8b	9d	10d
11d	12b	13a	14b	15b	16d	17b	18d	19b	20d
21a	22c	23d	24a	25d	26d	27a	28c	29d	30b

TEST 28

1b	2a	3d	4d	5a	6b	7d	8b	9c	10d
11c	12d	13b	14c	15c	16d	17a	18d	19a	20d
21b	22b	23c	24d	25a	26d	27c	28d	29d	30b

TEST 29

1d	2c	3c	4a	5b	6a	7d	8c	9a	10b
11d	12b	13b	14d	15a	16d	17b	18c	19b	20c
21b	22c	23a	24c	25d	26c	27b	28d	29a	30b

TEST 30

1b	2b	3d	4c	5c	6d	7a	8d	9a	10b
11d	12d	13d	14b	15a	16d	17b	18a	19c	20d
21c	22d	23b	24d	25a	26d	27d	28d	29c	30b

TEST 31

1b	2b	3b	4b	5b	6a	7c	8a	9a	10d
11d	12a	13c	14b	15a	16a	17b	18c	19b	20c
21c	22b	23d	24d	25d	26b	27d	28c	29c	30c

TEST 32

1a	2a	3c	4c	5d	6b	7a	8c	9b	10d
11d	12a	13d	14d	15d	16a	17d	18d	19d	20d
21d	22d	23c	24a	25c	26a	27b	28c	29d	30a

TEST 33

1a	2c	3d	4d	5d	6d	7c	8b	9b	10d
11c	12d	13c	14b	15b	16d	17d	18b	19a	20c
21a	22b	23a	24a	25b	26c	27d	28d	29b	30d

TEST 34

1b	2d	3a	4c	5d	6d	7b	8b	9d	10a
11c	12a	13d	14b	15d	16d	17d	18a	19b	20b
21c	22c	23d	24a	25b	26c	27d	28b	29d	30d

TEST 35

1d	2c	3b	4a	5a	6b	7d	8a	9b	10d
11d	12d	13b	14d	15a	16c	17c	18a	19b	20b
21c	22a	23b	24b	25a	26b	27d	28c	29a	30c

TEST 36

1a	2c	3a	4b	5c	6d	7d	8b	9d	10b
11a	12c	13d	14b	15d	16c	17c	18b	19c	20d
21d	22a	23d	24d	25d	26b	27d	28c	29d	30c

TEST 37

1b	2d	3c	4b	5a	6b	7c	8c	9a	10a
11a	12d	13b	14c	15c	16b	17a	18c	19b	20b
21c	22d	23a	24d	25d	26c	27b	28c	29c	30d

TEST 38

1a	2b	3d	4b	5b	6c	7c	8d	9d	10a
11a	12c	13d	14b	15d	16d	17d	18b	19c	20d
21b	22d	23b	24d	25a	26b	27d	28c	29b	30d

TEST 39

1d	2b	3a	4d	5a	6d	7c	8c	9c	10d
11a	12a	13d	14c	15a	16a	17d	18a	19d	20d
21d	22d	23c	24b	25b	26a	27b	28a	29d	30d

TEST 40

1d	2a	3b	4c	5d	6d	7d	8a	9a	10c
11a	12d	13b	14d	15d	16d	17d	18a	19b	20d
21c	22b	23b	24c	25b	26d	27a	28d	29c	30d

LITERATURA

- Adams, V. (1973) *An Introduction to Modern English Word-Formation.* London: Longman
- Aspinall, T. *et al*. (1999) *Advanced Masterclass CAE – Student's Book* (first published 1999, Eighth impression 2003). Oxford: Oxford University Press
- Aspinall, T. *et al*. (1999) *Advanced Masterclass CAE – Teacher`s Book* (Third impression 2000). Oxford: Oxford Uiniversity Press
- Aspinall, T. and Annette Capel (1999) *Advanced Masterclass CAE – Workbook with answers* (first published 1999; Fifth impression 2001). Oxford: Oxford University Press
- **A.Word.A.Day** Archives available at http://wordsmith.org/awad/wordlist.html 2004
- Ayto, J. (1999) *Twentieth Century Words* – The story of the new words in English over the last hundred years. Oxford, New York: Oxford University Press
- Bauer, L. (1983) *English Word-formation*. Cambridge: Cambridge University Press
- Bishop, G. *et al.* (2006) *Weird California*. New York: Sterling Publishing Co.
- Block, D. (1991) 'Some thoughts on DIY materials design', *ELT Journal* 45/3, 211-217
- Brumfit, C.J. ed. (1982) *English for International Communication*. Oxford: Pergamon Institute of English
- Carter, R. and M. McCarthy (1989) *Vocabulary and Language Teaching*. New York: Longman
- Dimitrijević, N. i K. Radovanović (2001a) *Test Your English*, Zbirka testova. Beograd: Plavi krug
- Dimitrijević, N. i K. Radovanović (2001b) *Test and Expand Your Vocabulary*, Zbirka testova. Beograd: Plavi krug
- Eastwood, J. (2003) *Oxford Practice Grammar* with answers (Second Edition). Oxford: Oxford University Press

- Fitikides, T.J. (2004) *Common Mistakes in English* with Exercises. Harlow, England: Pearson Education Limited – Longman
- Fleming, I. (1974) *Moonraker*. London: Pan Books Ltd.
- Gajić, R. (1985) 'Elementi analize englesko-srpskohrvatskih "lažnih parova"', *Prevodilac* 2/85, 41-46. Beograd: Udruženje naučnih i stručnih prevodilaca Srbije
- Gortan-Premk, D. (1990) 'Reč kao jedinica leksičkog sistema', *Prevodilac* 1-2/90, 21-24. Beograd: Udruženje naučnih i stručnih prevodilaca Srbije
- Grba, G., Karin Radovanović (2002) *Engleski jezik za IV razred gimnazije*, Dvanaesto izdanje. Beograd: Zavod za udžbenike i nastavna sredstva
- Gude, K. and Michael Duckworth (1994) *Proficiency Masterclass – Student`s Book* (Fifth impression 1995). Oxford: Oxford University Press
- Gude, K. and Michael Duckworth (2002) *Proficiency Masterclass – Student`s Book*. Oxford: Oxford University Press 2002
- Hall, N. and J. Shepheard (1993) *HELP with Words*. Oxford: Heinemann
- Harris, M. et al. (2002) *Opportunities Upper Intermediate – Students' Book* (first published 2002). London: Longman
- Harris, M. et al. (2002) *Opportunities Upper Intermediate – Language Powerbook* (first published 2002). London: Longman
- Hlebec, B. (1991) *Gramatika engleskog jezika za srednje škole*. Beograd: Zavod za udžbenike i nastavna sredstva
- House, R. et al. (2002) *Proficiency Masterclass – Teacher`s Book*. Oxford: Oxford University Press 2002
- Hurst, Rosalyn, M.A.Ed., Institute of Education, University of London (2001) *Seminar for state school teachers*, March 28-31, 2001 – skripta za seminar i usmena predavanja u prostorijama Britanskog saveta, Beograd
- Jančić, B. (1983) 'Književno i naučno-stručno prevođenje', *Prevodilac* 1/83, 19-30. Beograd: Udruženje naučnih i stručnih prevodilaca Srbije
- Kirkpatrick, B. (2002) *Book of Common Phrases* – Webster's Reference Library. New Lanark (Scotland): Geddes and Grosset
- Kostić, D. (1990) *Engineering English* – Izbor engleskih tekstova. Beograd: Univerzitet u Beogradu – Mašinski fakultet
- Kozák, J. (1973) *SHIPS – A concise guide in colour*. London: Hamlyn
- Lado, R. (1973) *Testovi u nastavi stranih jezika* (preveo s engleskog: Mladen Mihajlović). Beograd: Naučna knjiga
- Matthews, P. H. (1974) *Morphology. An Introduction to the Theory of Word Structure*. Cambridge: Cambridge University Press
- McCarthy, M. and F. O'Dell (2002) *English Vocabulary in Use – upper intermediate*. Cambridge: Cambridge University Press

- McCarthy, M. and F. O'Dell (2003) *English Vocabulary in Use – advanced*. Cambridge: Cambridge University Press
- Miller, G. A. (1991) *The Science of Words*. New York: Scientific American Library
- Milojević, J. (1996) *Gramatika reči – The Grammar of Words*. Beograd: Matematički institut SANU; Filološki fakultet
- Milojević, J. (2000) *Word and Words of English*. Belgrade: Papirus
- Milojević, J. (2003) *Essentials of English Morphology*. Belgrade: Papirus
- M.L.A. Standing Consultative Committee (1970) 'Reading in a Foreign Language', Report, *Modern Languages* LI/2, 60-61
- Mugglestone, P. (2002) *Opportunities Upper Intermediate – Teacher's Book* London: Longman
- Murphy, J. (2003) 'Task-based learning: the interaction between tasks and learners', *ELT Journal* 57/4, 352-360
- Nattinger, J. (1989) 'Some current trends in vocabulary teaching', in: *Vocabulary and Language Teaching*, eds. R. Carter and M. McCarthy, 62-82. New York: Longman
- O'Connell, S. (2002) *IELTS – International English Language Testing System – Student's Book* (Fifth impression 2004). Harlow (England): Longman/Pearson Education Limited
- *Opportunities Upper Intermediate* – Test Book (2002). London: Longman
- Partridge, E. (1960) *A Charm of Words*. London: Hamish Hamilton
- Partridge, E. (1961) *Adventuring among Words*. London: Andre Deutsch
- *Pocket Encyclopedia, The* (2001). UK: Geddes and Grosset
- Quirk, R. and Sidney Greenbaum (1975) *A University Grammar of English*, Third Impression. London: Longman Group Limited
- Redman, S. with E. Shaw (2002) *Vocabulary in Use – intermediate*, Self-study reference and practice for students of North American English. Cambridge: Cambridge University Press
- Sinclair, J. ed. (1993) *Collins COBUILD English Guides 2. Word Formation.* London: Collins
- Sinclair, J. ed. (1997) *Collins COBUILD English Guides 6. Homophones.* London: Collins
- Solomon, Ch. (1969) *Mathematics*. London: Hamlyn
- Swan, M. (1992) *Oxford Pocket Basic English Usage.* Oxford: Oxford University Press

ODABRANI REČNICI

- *Advanced Learner's Dictionary of Current English* (1972), A. S. Hornby *et al.*, London: Oxford University Press
- *American Century Dictionary* (1977), ed. L. Urdang, New York: Warner Books
- *American Heritage Dictionary of the English Language* (1976), ed. P. Davies, New York: Dell Publishing Co.
- *Architecture and Construction Words You Need* (1992), M. Horvatović, Smilja Novaković, Beograd: IŠP Savremena administracija
- Collins *Business English Dictionary* (1991), M. J. Wallace and Patrick J. Flynn, London: Collins
- *Enciklopediski englesko-srpskohrvatski rečnik* (1973), S. Ristić *et al.*, Beograd: Prosveta
- *Englesko-srpski frazeološki rečnik* (2001), M. Williams-Milosavljević i Boško Milosavljević, Beograd: Istočnik
- *Englesko-srpski frazeološki rečnik*, Treće izdanje (2003), Ž. Kovačević, Beograd: "Filip Višnjić"
- *Englesko-srpskohrvatski rečnik* (1975), Ristić S. i Živojin Simić, Beograd: Prosveta
- *Englesko-srpskohrvatski rečnik* (1978), M. Benson, Beograd: Prosveta
- *Englesko-srpskohrvatski rečnik drumskog saobraćaja* (1984), A. Fišer-Popović *et al.*, Beograd: IRO Rad
- *Englesko-srpskohrvatski VOJNI REČNIK* (1973), M.Popović, M. Četniković, Beograd: Vojnoizdavački zavod
- *English Duden Pictorial Dictionary* (1960), Manheim: Bibliographisches Institut
- *Essential* English-Serbian/Serbian-English Dictionary with notes on English and Serbian grammar – *Osnovni* englesko-srpski/srpsko-engleski rečnik sa engleskom i srpskom gramatikom (2003), B. Hlebec, Beograd: Zavod za udžbenike i nastavna sredstva
- *Financial Words You Need – Englesko-srpski rečnik finansijskih izraza* (1992), M. Cvejić, Beograd: IŠP Savremena administracija
- *Hemijsko-tehnološki rečnik*, *englesko-srpskohrvatski* (Drugo, dopunjeno izdanje) (1985), A. Mihailidi, Mihailo Mihailidi; Beograd: Privredni pregled
- *Hrvatsko ili srpsko-engleski rječnik privrednog nazivlja* (1978), V. Ivir, Zagreb: Školska knjiga
- *Leksikon stranih reči i izraza* (1980), M. Vujaklija, Beograd: Prosveta

- *Merriam-Webster pocket Dictionary of Synonyms* (1972), New York: Pocket Books
- *Naučno-tehnički REČNIK, englesko-srpskohrvatski,* IV izd. (1980), grupa autora, Beograd: Privredni pregled
- *New Horizon Ladder Dictionary of the English Language for Young Readers* (1970), J. R. Shaw with Janet Shaw, USA: Signet
- *Oxford Advanced Learner's Dictionary of Current English* (1990), ed. A. P. Cowie, Oxford: Oxford University Press
- *Oxford English Dictionary* (1970), eds. J. A. H. Murray *et. al.*, London: Oxford University Press
- *Privredno-poslovni rečnik* (1984), M. Landa, Beograd: Privredni pregled
- *Računarski rečnik – vodič za kompjuterski žargon* (1985), John Wedge, Beograd: NIRO Tehnička knjiga i Zavod za izdavanje udžbenika
- *Reader's Digest PRACTICAL DICTIONARY* (2007), ed. Anne Wevell, Cape Town: The Reader's Digest Association
- *Rečnik anglo-američkog slenga – A Dictionary of Anglo-American Slang* (2000), B. Gerzić, Beograd: Istar
- *Rečnik mašinske tehnike, srpskohrvatsko-engleski* (1986), J. Milićević, Beograd: Privredni pregled
- *Rečnik sinonima i antonima – englesko-srpskohrvatski i srpskohrvatsko- -engleski* (1986), 2. izdanje, J. Dajković, Beograd: Privredni pregled
- *Roget's new pocket Thesaurus in Dictionary Form* (1973), ed. N. Lewis, New York: Pocket Books
- *Srpsko-engleski frazeološki rečnik*, Drugo izdanje (2002), Ž. Kovačević, Beograd: „Filip Višnjić"
- *Srpsko-engleski rečnik engleskih frazalnih glagola* (2005), D. Đokić, Beograd: D. Đokić
- *Srpskohrvatsko-engleski rečnik* (1991), 3. izdanje, M. Benson, Beograd: Prosveta
- *Srpskohrvatsko-engleski GRAĐEVINSKI REČNIK* (1984), B. Vukićević, Beograd: IRO Građevinska knjiga
- *Standard Serbian-English Dictionary* with notes on Serbian grammar – *Standardni srpsko-engleski rečnik* sa engleskom gramatikom (2003), B. Hlebec, Beograd: Zavod za udžbenike i nastavna sredstva
- *Rečnik računarskih termina, englesko-srpskohrvatski* (1986), V. Tasić, Beograd: NIRO Tehnička knjiga i Zavod za udžbenike i nastavna sredstva
- *Veliki rečnik stranih reči i izraza* (2006), I. Klajn, Milan Šipka; Novi Sad: Prometej
- *Webster's Concise English Thesaurus* (2002), Scotland: Geddes and Grosset

ELEKTRONSKI REČNICI

- *Cambridge Advanced Learner's Dictionary* on CD ROM (2003), Version 1.0, Cambridge University Pres
- *Cambridge International Dictionary of English* on CD ROM (2001), Cambridge University Press
- *Longman Dictionary of Contemporary English* on CD ROM (2003), Pearson Education Ltd.
- *Merriam-Webster On-line* – The Language Center: www.m-w.com/
- *Oxford GENIE* – (Oxford Advanced Learner's Dictionary of Current English, Sixth Edition) – Oxford University Press 2003
- *The American Heritage Dictionary of the English Language*, on-line site: www.bartleby.com/61

CIP - Каталогизација у публикацији
Народна библиотека Србије, Београд

811.111'276.6:62(075.8)

ЈОВАНОВИЋ, Слободан Д., 1954-
Engleski jezik za studente tehnike :
izbor tekstova i testova za usvajanje
vokabulara / Slobodan D. Jovanović. - 2.
izd., izmenjeno i dopunjeno. - Beograd :
Visoka tehnička škola strukovnih studija,
2010 (Beograd : Klasa). - 184 str. ; 23 cm

Tiraž 200. - Bibliografija: str. 178-183.

ISBN 978-86-86691-27-9

a) Енглески језик - Техничка терминологија
COBISS.SR-ID 176414220

www.ingramcontent.com/pod-product-compliance
Lightning Source LLC
Chambersburg PA
CBHW060239050426
42448CB00009B/1522